How Our Society Fuels Exhaustion
and How to Set Yourself Free

BURNOUT HIGHWAY

ANMOL DIDDAN

Behavioral & Culture Researcher,
Coach & Consultant, Google Alum

RIVER GROVE
BOOKS

This publication is designed to provide accurate and authoritative information in regard to the subject matter covered. It is sold with the understanding that the publisher and author are not engaged in rendering legal, accounting, or other professional services. Nothing herein shall create an attorney-client relationship, and nothing herein shall constitute legal advice or a solicitation to offer legal advice. If legal advice or other expert assistance is required, the services of a competent professional should be sought.

Published by River Grove Books
Austin, TX
www.gbgpress.com

Distributed by River Grove Books

Design and composition by Greenleaf Book Group and Shraddha Gandhi, Chashmaagraph
Cover design by Shraddha Gandhi, Chashmaagraph

Publisher's Cataloging-in-Publication data is available.

Print ISBN: 979-8-90052-010-0

eBook ISBN: 979-8-90052-011-7

First Edition

To all the people, paths, and places that enabled this perspective, thank you.

CONTENTS

Foreword—Saurabh Dangwal vii

Introduction 1

Part 1: The Trails That Became the Burnout Highway

   1 The Rise of Capitalistic Society 19

   2 Global Capital, Local Labor 39

   3 The Education System 57

   REST STOPS

   Define Your Career Ikigai 82
   Make Your Values Your Anchor 87

Part 2: Modernity Widens the Burnout Highway

   4 Expectation vs. Reality for Millennials 99

   5 Corporate Structures and Mass Job Creation. . 113

   6 One-Size-Fits-All Approach to Work 139

   REST STOPS

   Choose People, Not Jobs! 166
   Empower Yourself with Vulnerability 169

Part 3: The Mental Toll of the Burnout Highway

   7 The Inner Child That Controls You 177

   8 The Demonization of Rest 193

   9 A Decline of the Collective 217

REST STOPS

Talk to Strangers! 228
Build a Conscious Relationship with Technology. . 232
Embrace the Power of Incrementality and Care . . 235
Be Curious, Not Judgmental about Yourself 244

Conclusion: You Can't Ride a Bike without
Riding a Bike 249

Acknowledgments 259

Notes. 261

About the Author 277

FOREWORD

I first met Anmol in 2017, when I hired him onto my team at Google. Over the past eight years, I've had the privilege of managing him, learning from him, and building a lasting friendship. I often joked he was me, just ten years younger. Though our paths unfolded in different countries, the frustrations of the conventional corporate track felt remarkably similar.

These parallel journeys kept us connected, as we spent years exchanging ideas about rediscovering passion, breaking away from convention, and finding the courage to take new roads when the familiar ones no longer worked for us.

As someone who grew up in India, moved to Singapore, and followed the rhythm of a traditional nine-to-five career, I know what burnout feels like. At the time, I didn't have the language for it—it was simply exhaustion, the sense of being "always on." But beneath that, I was a quietly restless rebel:

questioning the traditional education, corporate culture, and paths society conditions us to accept.

Even today, my parents worry when I don't have a "job" in the traditional sense. Watching my father work at the same office for 25 years instilled in me a fear of ending up the same way. Ironically, I still spent two decades in offices—leading teams at companies like Google, Spotify, and Yahoo!, among others. I was perhaps using variety as a crutch—a stark contrast to the stability that drove my father.

When I read *Burnout Highway*, one thought stayed with me: I could have chosen differently, sooner, if I had been a bit more aware of how my context shaped me. I could have perhaps been a bit braver, and more willing to follow what felt true to me.

That cycle of vulnerability, awareness, acknowledgment, and action is at the heart of both Anmol's journey and mine. And it is the essence of *Burnout Highway*. This is not a reckless call to abandon responsibilities or ignore the realities of life. Instead, it is an invitation to recognize signs of burnout, giving yourself permission to pull over at a rest stop when needed, and to choose a path that feels true, via compassion and practical rationality.

When Anmol first told me he was writing this book, I didn't picture a manuscript. I pictured one of our WhatsApp threads—weaving between life updates, sharp one-liners, career meltdowns, and spontaneous dreams of escape. In a way, *Burnout Highway* feels like a codification of our texts over a decade.

We've never spoken about burnout as a clinical condition, but as a road we've both travelled: headlights dim, the tank near empty, convinced the next fuel stop was just one more step up the ladder. It wasn't.

That is what makes *Burnout Highway* so powerful. It is not theoretical. It is not a made-up list of "10 easy steps to fix burnout." It is a collection of road-tested lessons, born of lived and observed experience, refined through honest, vulnerable conversation.

Burnout Highway reframes burnout as more than just individual exhaustion; it is a predictable outcome of how our society is structured and incentivized. This makes burnout a shared reality, not an individual failure of resilience. The good news is Anmol's insights can help you reframe the conversation in your own life, enabled by an empowering reflection of your own decisions, toward a more emotionally sustainable path. Ultimately, you can also contribute to creating emotionally sustainable teams, workplaces, and communities.

Reading this book feels like having Anmol in the passenger seat—he's there to point out bends you don't see, remind you when to take an exit for a breather, and occasionally turn up the music when words aren't enough. He is candid about the potholes, generous with the shortcuts, and clear that the "right highway" isn't the same for everyone.

If you've ever found yourself "behind the wheel," wondering whether to keep driving or stop altogether, this book is for you. It is not just a map. It is a companion—proof that everyone has been where you are, and a reminder that you can still get to wherever you need to be.

—Saurabh Dangwal

INTRODUCTION

I t took me about three years to realize I was burned out. At the time, I was leading a team of behavioral researchers at Google. I had started with the company in 2012, making my way up the corporate ladder in different roles and functions to my current position. I'd also had the opportunity to work in three continents, across India, Ireland, Singapore, and New York.

Through my corporate career, I always tried to be motivated by the right incentive, which in my mind was learning through experience. I prioritized personal growth and learning through diverse professional experiences while many around me solely prioritized an upward, monetary trajectory. I took the company at face value when they asked me "to bring my whole self" to work, not buying into the corporate dance required for rapid vertical growth. But, as I progressed up the ladder, the promise of fulfilling work didn't really materialize.

I didn't immediately recognize the general exhaustion I constantly felt as the first feelings of burnout. And the exhaustion was accompanied by a deep sense of guilt.

My early context had been that of a humble, middle-class Indian boy with a constant family struggle for money. We never had enough of it and when we did, there was a large family at the table, each clamoring for a pile. It was a childhood of looking at adults from afar and concluding that money was the only way out. And a conclusion that a "dream job" was the only ticket out of that existence. Which I apparently now had. However, my career felt emotionally unsustainable.

I yo-yoed a lot between a deep sense of gratitude for my life and a deep sense of regretful contempt. The feeling of being lucky always followed, and a voice constantly yelled, "Impostor!" I found myself thinking about the what-ifs of an alternate existence, one that would have been built around my true passions, a constant pining to experience that alternate reality.

It was a never-ending cycle of exhaustion, trying to look at the bright side, and back to exhaustion again. Every email, every ping, every comment on a work document, every little task in my life felt like Mount Everest. I tried seeking help through the many channels of support my immensely supportive company offered me. These things provided temporary relief, but that feeling of having to climb Everest to send an email after yet another week off always lurked around the corner.

I constantly pondered about what drove me there, in what seemed like a general burnout epidemic around me, at one of the most economically prosperous companies in history. One of my qualities has been that I can talk to people and truly be vulnerable. And I brought that to the workplace, vehemently, and, at times, unnecessarily so. That meant I knew of more people suffering like I was suffering, trapped in a life they couldn't give up, while romanticizing the escape.

Why was I and so many of my colleagues on this burnout highway with seemingly no way off?

What Is Burnout?

In 2019, the World Health Organization defined burnout as "a syndrome conceptualized as resulting from chronic workplace stress that has not been successfully managed. It is characterized by three dimensions: (1) feelings of energy depletion or exhaustion; (2) increased mental distance from one's job, or feelings of negativism or cynicism related to one's job; and (3) a sense of ineffectiveness and lack of accomplishment."[1]

The average person in the United States, based on Bureau of Labor Statistics data of an average 35-hour workweek, through their lifetime spends about a third of their life at work, or about 90,000 hours.[2] More so, various studies put the percentage of workers in America reporting that they hated their job between 50 percent and 80 percent. Let's pause here and think about that for a minute. Nearly four out of five workers in America, the pinnacle of the modern industrial world, are okay admitting that.

So, if you do the math, about a third of the average worker's life is spent somewhere they might hate. Another third would be spent sleeping, and finally, another third being old. There it goes, the gift of life feeling like a curse in a cubicle.

The acceleration of burnout has been alarming, with each generation facing "peak stress" earlier in their lives. According to a 2023 survey by Zippia, 89 percent of Americans reported feeling burned out within the past year.[3] In 2022, this was at 59 percent and a year earlier it was 13.5 percent. Research conducted by Future Forum in 2022 shows that of the 10,243 full-time desk-based workers polled in six countries including the United States and the United Kingdom, over 40 percent said they were burned out.[4]

The rate of burnout appears to be much starker in the developed world, even with the higher standard of living, welfare, and self-actualization. When we look at Google Trends search data for the search topic "burnout," it becomes clear that there is higher interest across the developed world. In the last five years, the regions showing the highest search interest are countries across Western Europe—Austria, Switzerland, Germany, the Netherlands, Sweden, and Belgium. Additionally, countries like Canada and Australia also show relatively high search interest for "burnout" compared to places in Asia or Latin America.[5] These developed nations are among the richest, most welfare-driven, high-standard-of-living states in the world.

In the East, burnout is often looked at through the lens of Western cultures being extremely materialistic and thus unable to attain happiness. However, many Eastern countries have wholly embraced consumerism, even in economies that claim to be socialist in principle. Thus, even in the East, people are seeking happiness through materialism itself, even more obsessively so, as developing economies start from a lower base. So, attempting to view burnout and general unhappiness in the world through the lens of culture wars is a fallacy, to say the least.

The 75-plus years since World War II have been the most peaceful and prosperous time for humanity based on average per capita incomes, lifetime expectancy, literacy, and any other developmental metric. Yet, it feels like we're living in an exhausted, emotionally unsustainable world, bombarded by information—distracted, busy, frantic even, yet feeling unaccomplished. We all seem a bit restless, frenzied, seeking solutions on screens to problems created by our minds.

One positive is the increasingly genuine awareness and effort around addressing mental health challenges like burnout. We've made strides as a global community toward creating a more positive environment and discourse around burnout and mental health. Never before have we lived in a world where being depressed, anxious, or just not feeling up to it is this okay and accepted. And that's good; it is a start.

However, we haven't helped people understand the interplay of their contexts and the incentive structures within which they live their lives, toward empowering mental health.

"Treating" Burnout

We live in an individualistic world, one where people feel empowered through agency. People like to believe that their lives can be designed exactly as they want, in the vacuum of their own bubbles. While that is largely true, the importance of the role of the collective in the path our lives end up traversing is often underappreciated. This prevents people from designing emotionally sustainable lives and careers.

Truth is, no matter what path your life takes, it is a result of a long-drawn intertwining of the context within which you live your life—culture, systems, family, technology, and incentives that defined your path, one way or another.

However, the solutions around how we view and treat burnout and mental health in general are often tactical, focused on support and intervention—the *what*—at an individual level.

While such solutions are critical to recovery, they don't tend to touch on the systems and structures that have made mental health struggles far too common—the *why* behind these increasingly common experiences.

I find that a bit surprising, as a remedial intervention usually needs to involve some form of mindfulness of the deeper why to begin with. And the basis of mindfulness is awareness, of the good, bad, and ugly. While there is an emphasis on such awareness at an individual level, there is a lack of emphasis on awareness of how the context of our lives and systemic incentives affect the individual.

If you Google "best books on burnout," here are its usual top results:

- *Burnout, the Secret to Unlocking the Stress Cycle*
- *HBR Guide to Beating Burnout*
- *Understanding Workplace Burnout*
- *Burnout Recovery—15 Steps*
- *The Burnout Solution*
- *The Burnout Fix*
- *Neuro-Habits—Rewire Your Brain for Self-Defeating Behaviors and Make the Right Choice Every Time*
- *Beating Burnout at Work*

Read through this list again and make a mental note of what you observe in the titles—we'll come back to it later.

What Marketing Taught Me about Burnout

As a consumer insights professional at Google, I had endless conversations around the purchase funnel or purchase journey for consumers with brands. It is used in every marketing plan, in some form. There are different versions of the funnel, but the simplistic Awareness, Interest, Consideration, Action funnel for a consumer or brand can give us an insight into how we structure problems and needs as humans. The brand tries to tweak its marketing and media delivery for consumers who are going through these stages, or, at times, skipping or boomeranging between stages.

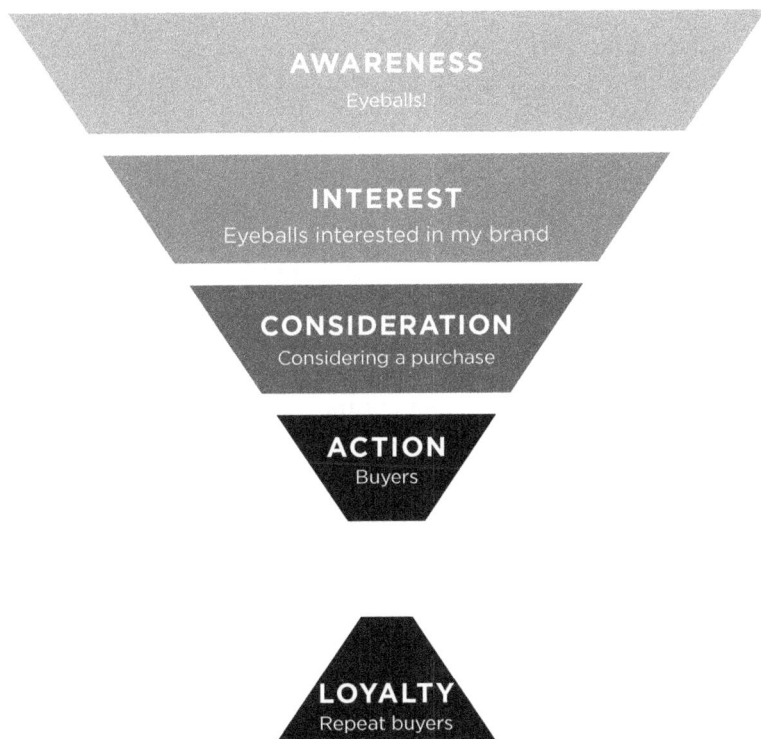

AWARENESS
Eyeballs!

INTEREST
Eyeballs interested in my brand

CONSIDERATION
Considering a purchase

ACTION
Buyers

LOYALTY
Repeat buyers

The brand marketing funnel

While consumer journeys have gotten a lot less linear since the advent of the smartphone, this funnel still works for every brand since it helps break down their entire audience and consumer base who are in different mindsets at different stages for a need they're trying to solve.

If you use car buying as an example, your car buying journey started from the realization of a need for a new car. You could have seen some ads on TV for a few brands that caught your attention and made you aware of them. You then went onto their websites to check features and so on to generate further interest. You then reached out to two or three dealerships to set up test drives and understand promotional offers to build your consideration set. Finally, you reached the action of buying a car, and maybe you liked it so much you were a loyal customer, buying another one for someone in your family from the same brand.

You were solving a different need at every stage of this funnel, and the brand you bought probably guided you through these need stages, each of which were important, for both you and the brand. While different brands have different marketing goals, generally speaking, brands value consumers closer to action and, depending on the industry, really value loyalty (think credit cards or airlines). Why? Simply because the number of people buying your product will always be much smaller than the number of people aware of your brand.

The point of this marketing lesson is that humans solve all needs in such a manner, and this is true for mental health needs too. However, the focus of a lot of mental health–related self-help in the world today is based on intervention and not awareness—a tactical approach. The funnel is almost flipped when it comes to our approach to mental health.

This is because when people aren't feeling up to it, they naturally focus on feeling better quickly and only over the long term, with a lot of work, do they understand or stumble upon the deeper cause of their feelings in the first place. This is not because of any deep-state propaganda, but rather simply what makes sense, both for the patient and practitioner.

However, digging deep and uncovering that insight, which lies both at an individual and collective level, will help us deal with the virus at its source. Often, this is not the approach for a lot of people, who boomerang in and out of mental health issues without understanding the root causes of their patterns. Your patterns are a combination of the contexts you existed within, the systems that governed your life, and the quirks that made you, you!

The larger why is often hardest to change for an individual. Thus, awareness of that has a lesser focus in approaches to mental health challenges. For example, how did cultural or systemic aspects affect your mental health?

AWARE
of the deeper why

CONSIDERING
*making a positive change
to address mental health challenges*

More people tend to be in these stages when it comes to their mental health.

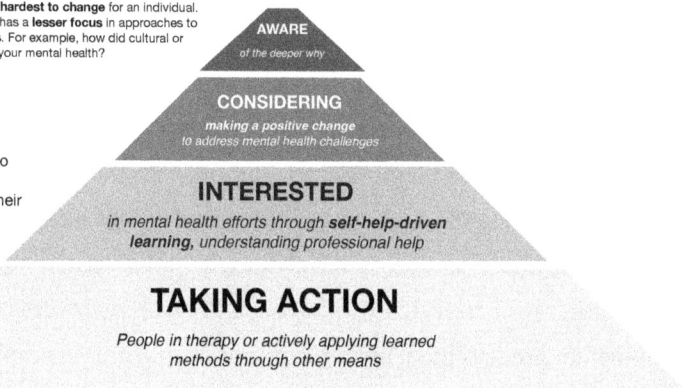

INTERESTED
*in mental health efforts through **self-help-driven
learning**, understanding professional help*

TAKING ACTION
*People in therapy or actively applying learned
methods through other means*

The flipped "burnout or mental health funnel"

When you look at this through the lens of burnout in the corporate world, the nature of discourse around rising burnout rates in the upper echelons is often wrapped in a warm, fuzzy blanket of the increasing tactical support that is provided to employees. While it is true that support is increasing and necessary, it is also a distraction from digging deeper into systemic challenges in the corporate workplace and the individual corporate experience.

Let's return to the book titles on burnout. What stood out for you? For me, through the research for this book, I saw two themes emerging generally in mental health–related self-help books and, specifically, in the books on burnout:

(1) While the advice is excellent and important, the focus is on actions an individual can take to treat burnout. This individual approach is, of course, important and empowering; however, systemic causal factors are given less importance, whether at work or beyond. Like most collective experiences, there are structural reasons behind this increasingly common experience, and the awareness of that is generally missing in the approach to recovering from burnout.

(2) Self-help for burnout today takes an academic approach to a practical problem. There was only so much neuroscience that could help me make sense of my real-world experiences. We don't see practical takes on burnout, based on paths and experiences in the corporate or real world. Probably because corporate workers are too busy trying to build corporate careers!

In my mind, there had to be better explanations for this deeply individual, yet increasingly collective experience.

A Systemic Approach

So far, we've had a rather simplistic take on burnout, but the urgency of the situation demands that change. Feeling debilitatingly burned out comes not just from your immediate experience at work. The factors that drive someone to such stifling burnout have many, often less understood personal, experiential, and contextual factors at play, extending far beyond work to the constructs of society itself.

Focusing simply on a tactical, symptomatic approach to burnout or mental health in general confirms a mental narrative of self-blame, of it being your own fault, boomeranging through emotions with self-contempt, burdening yourself with toxic self-talk, and hoping for miraculous tactical "fixes." But tactical fixes only go so far when a foundational awareness and understanding of root causes is missing.

No matter the cocktail that gets one there, burnout is deeply intertwined with our experiences at work, and, more specifically, our ability to be functional at future work. And, according to US labor data, as of 2025, for about 60 percent of Americans[6] that experience at work is defined by a job or a corporate experience.

In the corporate world, burnout is often disguised in statements like "needing a change" or "a lack of growth" or "a new challenge." Even though strides have been made, a healthy discourse around burnout is lacking in many companies. Best case, it is usually dealt with through isolation and support of the employee, leading to some feelings of shame when they return, and worst case, through termination. This approach distracts from delving deeper into what causes burnout, beyond the individual to the collective and systemic level, which extends beyond the workplace to the setup of our society in general.

In Buddhism or generally in meditation practices, there is an emphasis on awareness. Awareness of the impermanence of life, of its discomforts, of its wonders and its drivers. That is the first step toward finding acceptance, of everything that comes your way, including the inevitable suffering that is part of being human, which will lead to a deeper understanding and a new dawn. Buddha's first noble truth can be summarized as, "Life is suffering," and we suffer more than we need to because we try to constantly alleviate that suffering.

I wanted to explore and better understand this deeply individual yet increasingly collective suffering, through my experience and the experiences of so many others, aiming to make people aware of how they got here. I began working on this book after I was laid off from Google in 2023 along with 12,000-plus fellow employees as part of the ongoing, massive tech layoffs. This book is as much about self-discovery as it is about understanding the larger context that runs all our lives— the context of the systems within which we make decisions, the milestones we were taught to desire, and the feelings of fulfillment we thought they ought to provide. And how those systems set many of us up for burnout.

Like most of my career in behavioral research, my experience, my network, and websites like Google, Wikipedia, Britannica, and the many open research papers available online are my tools for this book. I have also supplemented my interpretations through a group survey with over 50 former colleagues to gain a more practical understanding of burnout in the corporate world, based in real-world experience. The survey comprised corporate workers and founders across India, the US, Australia, Canada, Hong Kong, Singapore, Hungary, Germany, Kenya, Spain, and the UK between the ages of 24 and 55, with six to more than 25 years of experience. Tellingly, 74 percent of the group reported feeling burned out some or all of the time. Only 5 percent reported not ever feeling burned out.

While this book focuses on burnout through the lens of an average corporate experience in today's world, it's primarily a story of the systems and structures that got us here, looking at early principles the industrial revolution and colonization put in place, the nature of capital and labor, education systems, corporate structures, the rise of desk labor, and the outburst of technology in our lives.

As you read this book, think about your relationship with work: Why do you do what you do? What role does money play in your life? How do you prefer to work? Concurrently, think about the work you do in the context of the broader social and economic structures in which you exist:

Is the setup of our lives misleading? Or have we outgrown systems and structures that were designed to deliver outcomes we no longer deem emotionally favorable? Are we just more open to admitting it when we are struggling? Are the incentive structures in society stacked against individual happiness? Were we ever trying to find happiness?

Pondering such existential questions may be a luxury for many of us in the trenches, but to truly empower ourselves as workers, we need to build an awareness and understanding of the incentives that systems and corporations respond to. We need to understand the story of capitalism, our systems, and corporations, and their impact on our lives. Most importantly, we need to understand that individuals with burnout can recover by attaching less blame to themselves, with compassion and an awareness of the systems they navigated.

While this is not a self-help book in the traditional sense, I do include several practical tactics and techniques that have helped me move forward in my journey out of burnout—including changing my attitude toward work, reexamining my relationship with money or perceived needs, and reconnecting with others and with nature. These tactics are included in each section as "rest stops," if you will, to help you as you work to get off the burnout highway.

PART
ONE

THE RISE OF
CAPITALISTIC
SOCIETY

THE TRAILS THAT BECAME THE

BURNOUT HIGHWAY

GLOBAL CAPITAL, LOCAL LABOR

THE EDUCATION SYSTEM

CHAPTER 1

The Rise of Capitalistic Society

Anything systemic today cannot be analyzed without the larger context of capitalism, the overarching system that runs our political economy and all our lives. This is true for burnout as well, especially burnout in the corporate context as larger incentives in society, and the corporate experience, were put in place by capitalistic principles.

While there are many accepted definitions of capitalism, today the term relates to the free market or the free enterprise economy, dominant in the Western world. It was key to breaking up the archaic feudal systems prevalent across the world before the industrial revolution. It is characterized by private ownership of capital and production, and income is usually guided by market forces. Most countries today have some form of capitalism that makes up the basis of their economies, including countries like Russia, China, and India that are, in principle, communist or socialist.

While capitalism lifted millions out of poverty and created the conditions for the innovative, technologically driven world we live in today, it is designed to disproportionately benefit owners of capital. I say this with a pinch of salt, as someone who has greatly benefited from global capitalism as "labor," catapulting myself from one of the poorest states in India to living in four countries across three continents all before the age of 30. Thus, I am by no means anti-capitalism. I am pro-awareness, of how it works, of its incentives for the capitalists, the labor, and its primary vehicle—the corporation. This awareness helps you at an individual level set the right expectations as a micro-cog within this large capitalistic wheel.

In a world where increasingly corporations feel like countries, at an individual level, building an awareness of the intricacies of capitalism is the beginning of finding your oasis within it. This can help empower you mentally to improve both your individual and collective corporate experience. To understand why burnout has become so pervasive, we first need to understand how our modern capitalist system came to be and how it has evolved. Let's go back to the very beginning of this stage in the history of our world, to a time when the global corporation was still an idea.

Mercantilism and Colonization

Our current form of capitalism was driven by a single invention—the stock markets. It all started in March 1602 when the Dutch East India company established the world's first stock exchange and traded shares in Amsterdam.[1] The Amsterdam stock exchange still exists today as a part of Euronext, a pan-European stock exchange. I remember being spellbound looking at the building where it all began in central Amsterdam during my first visit there in 2013, wondering if those first traders had any idea of how this would transform the world forever. I make it a point to stroll by the building and ruminate every time I'm in Amsterdam.

While Amsterdam was the first formally recognized stock exchange in the world, according to various historians, state loan stocks had been negotiated in Venice, Florence, and Genoa before 1328.[2] Thus, flourishing pockets of capitalism have existed in Europe since the Middle Ages and it is the birthplace of the idea of capitalism.

It took over a century to get the second stock exchange in Paris in 1724 followed by Philadelphia in 1790. This explains why the Dutch Empire had a head start colonizing the world. The first three decades of the 19th century saw stock exchanges popping up across London (1801), Milan (1808), New York (1817), Frankfurt (1820), and Madrid (1831). Toronto (1852) and the Bombay Stock Exchange (1875) followed in the second half of the 19th century. Notice the concentration of stock exchanges across Europe and North America, showcasing the late adoption of this way of economic life in Asia, Africa, and Latin America.

But what did the stock exchange actually do? For the first time, it enabled collective ownership of private enterprise, driven by anyone in principle, not just the kings and feudal lords. In the context of the time, this newfound ability to efficiently accumulate and allocate excess public capital toward intensive technological improvements gave Europeans the economic might to go out and colonize the world, for textiles, spices, and anything else they could get their hands on, transferring disproportionate wealth back to Europe. This cycle of capital accumulation works in the same way today, just at a much larger scale, across thousands of companies. Effective capital allocation is probably the most efficient outcome of capitalism.

Back then, this newfound public capital bestowed European powers with huge resources to continuously innovate through cartography, shipbuilding, and global expeditions to conquer (exploit) the world. This way of life fostered an expansive mindset, one that made Europe look to distant parts of the world for capital accumulation and wealth transfer. It was the first time Europeans invested in economically fruitful activities all over the world, rather than economically unproductive enterprises like cathedrals back home. It formed the foundation of the modern world and the transfer of wealth from India, China, Latin America, and the Far East to Europe, creating a north-south developmental divide in the world that runs to this day.

This thirst for wealth was consistent with the policies of European mercantilist states that were practiced through the 16th to 18th centuries. Mercantilism promoted governmental regulation of a nation's economy for the purpose of increasing a nation's power at the expense of rival national powers. It led to the creation of monopolistic trading companies like the Dutch, French, and British East India Companies that became the vehicles of plunder of the colonies, existing solely to supply resources back to the mother countries in Europe. Commercial rivalries between these powers also led to military conflict, notably the three Anglo-Dutch wars in the 17th and 18th centuries.

The term "mercantilism" was coined by the Scottish economist Adam Smith in his book *The Wealth of Nations* (1776).[3] The basis of mercantilism was a nation's precious metals or natural resources in general, such as gold and silver, or oil and energy today. These were deemed critical to a nation's wealth. If a nation did not possess mines or have access to them, for example, precious metals must be obtained by trade or colonialism. It essentially led to the scramble for energy security that forms the basis of today's economies.

Mercantilism also advocated for trade balances to be favorable—an excess of exports over imports, a principle that applies to this day through the foundational concept of a trade deficit and a country's balance of payments. This concept has become all too familiar in the first few months of President Trump's second term.

Colonial possessions were to serve as markets for exports and as suppliers of raw materials to the mother country, buying expensive finished articles from the mother country, after having traded raw materials to it for next to nothing. Manufacturing was forbidden in colonies, and all commerce between the colony and mother country was held to be a monopoly of the mother country. This created a rapidly steady, outward drain of resources from the colonial economy to the mother economy.

A strong nation, according to mercantilism, was to have a large population, as that provides steady supplies of labor, soldiers, and consumers. Human wants were to be minimized, especially for imported luxury goods, for they drained off precious foreign exchange. Laws regulating food and drugs were to be passed to make sure that wants were held low. Parsimony was regarded as a virtue, for only by these means could capital be created and deployed within the economy. An Economics 101 concept taught today is the equilibrium between investments, savings, and consumption in an economy, which stems from these mercantilist principles.

In effect, mercantilism provided a favorable climate for the early development of capitalism, with savings driving investments, consumption, and large profits. And these principles still govern the modern world today.

The beacon of this modern capitalistic world, the US, deploys a largely mercantilist playbook, securing energy resources globally, using the dollar as a peg for other currencies, and being the most efficient in the world at transferring and deploying its savings as investments (or capital) into its historically deep financial markets. While the dollar as a peg for other currencies might slowly change as America goes through an economic policy shift to try to promote domestic manufacturing, this still holds true.

Thus, the foundation of capitalism has always been based in a form of exploitation, of both the colonies (suppliers) and the labor/soldiers within the mother country, with the labor in the home country getting a deal that is much better than in the exploited colonies. However, the true winners were the corporations that became the vehicles of mercantilism, and the mercantilist states, whose fortunes became increasingly intertwined with corporations.

The Foundations of Corporate Labor

The Dutch East India Company was established by the States General of the Netherlands amalgamating existing companies into the first joint-stock company in the world, granting it a 21-year monopoly to carry out trade activities in Asia. Shares in the company could be bought by any resident of the Dutch United Provinces and then subsequently bought and sold in open-air secondary markets.

It is sometimes considered to have been the first truly multinational corporation. It was a powerful company possessing quasi-governmental powers, including the ability to wage war, imprison and execute convicts, negotiate treaties, strike its own coins, and establish colonies.

Statistically, it eclipsed all its rivals in the Asia trade. Between 1602 and the end of the 18th century, the company sent almost a million Europeans to work in the Asia trade on 4,785 ships, and netted for their efforts more than 2.5 million tons of Asian trade goods. By contrast, the rest of Europe combined sent just 882,412 people from 1500 to 1795, and the fleet of the English East India Company, their nearest competitor, was a distant second to its total traffic, with 2,690 ships carrying a mere one-fifth the tonnage of goods.[4] The Dutch East India Company enjoyed huge profits from its spice monopoly through most of the 17th century.[5]

Having been set up in 1602 to profit from the Malukan (Malacca) spice trade, the company established a capital in the port city of Jayakarta (Jakarta) in 1609 and changed its name to Batavia. Over the next two centuries the company acquired additional ports as trading bases and safeguarded their interests by taking over surrounding territory, as far as Sri Lanka. Sri Lanka remained an important trading concern and paid an 18 percent annual dividend for almost 200 years.

This playbook was used by every European colonial power

across Asia, Africa, and South America, regions that were not yet concerned with the unending accumulation and transfer of wealth, something they would eventually have to sign up to as they became independent nations.

To understand how early capitalism and these companies looked at labor in general, we need to look at the setup of both the colonies and the mother countries.

The elephant in the room here is enslavement, which often is described and acknowledged as an American evil in today's world. In fact, it skyrocketed in the 16th century as a by-product of colonialism, something Europeans generally tend to ignore.

According to various historians, slavery was institutionalized as early as 3500 BC in the Mesopotamian civilization and practiced in different forms across Asia, Africa, the Middle East, and Europe.[6] However, beginning in the 16th century, European merchants, starting mainly in Portugal, initiated the transatlantic slave trade. They mostly purchased imprisoned Africans (and exported commodities including gold and ivory) from West African kingdoms, transporting them to Europe's colonies in the Americas. The merchants were sources of desired goods including guns, gunpowder, copper, and cloth, and this demand for imported goods drove local wars and other means to the enslavement of Africans in ever greater numbers. While enslavement isn't actively practiced today, this story plays out far too often in developing economies to this day.

In India and throughout the colonies, people were forced into slavery to create the local workforce. Alongside Russians, Afghans, Mongol Oirds, and Shia Iranians, Indian slaves were an important component of the highly active slave markets of medieval and modern Asia. The reason Indian and Asian slaves weren't as widespread in the West was because slaves from Asia, and in particular India, fetched higher prices in the medieval world. This was due to the fact that Asia, and in particular India, was a leader in textiles, architecture, and art, which meant that slaves from these parts fetched higher prices as compared to their African counterparts—a sort of market signaling if you will.

Thus, while European colonialism cannot be blamed for the birth of slavery, it has to bear a large burden for its globalization.

Understanding this first wave of "globalization" can help us understand the bedrocks of corporate existence today. Delving deeper into the early attitudes of the East India Companies toward labor in the colonies gives us insight into how they went about colonizing areas of Africa, Asia, and Latin America.

A 2001 paper by American economists Daron Acemoglu, Simon Johnson, and James Robinson explores how perceived mortality rates and exposure to disease affected policies within colonies and the reasons for variance in per capita incomes in European colonies across Asia, Africa, North America, and Australia/New Zealand.[7]

They say, at one extreme, European powers set up "extractive states" exemplified by the Belgian colonization of Congo. European powers in these extractive states did not have any emphasis on institutions, private property, and the settling of Europeans in these colonies. The sole focus was to transfer resources from these states back to Europe, using cheap domestic labor and resources they could exploit.

At the other extreme, where conditions were more favorable

to Europeans, colonists migrated to these colonies creating what the historian Alfred Crosby coined as "Neo-Europes."[8] The settlers tried to emulate European institutions in these colonies, examples of which include Canada, the US, Australia, and New Zealand, where freedom struggles involved the European migrant demanding to be rid of their European masters, without the consultation of the Indigenous peoples of those lands.

This affected the adoption of labor codes and laws across extractive colonies long after most of these countries gained independence. In Latin America, those reforms typically occurred a century after the countries gained independence. In Africa they were usually introduced at the end of the colonial period, as late as the 1970s.

But because the economy was concentrated in a few privileged firms and sectors, and because those who had the capacity to mobilize also worked there, the labor laws only applied in those sectors. Enforcing such a complex labor code on small production units was both unfeasible and economically disruptive, something we still see in the "sweatshops" that exist across Asia and Africa.

Labor in the Mother Country

While slavery and the foundational exploitation of labor in colonies by mercantilist states/companies is one aspect of the early capitalists' view on labor, the more relevant aspect is the treatment of labor and soldiers in the mother country. This gives us a more fundamental understanding of early attitudes toward labor by capitalists or corporations and is more reflective of the large corporation's principles in its attitude toward its employees today.

During the 1600s, as European colonies undertook expeditions to create "extractive states," Europe itself was going through a positively disruptive period, laying the groundwork for the industrial revolution. Populations of most major European countries increased 50–100 percent across the 17th and 18th centuries. This was driven by a boom in agriculture through crops like potatoes, leading to greater food security, reduction in mortality rates, and increased adoption of technology through a scientific mindset that accompanied the Renaissance, which was at its peak.

This meant that more people needed to be put to work, and a continent already booming with merchants, attuned to market transactions, and flooded with new resources provided the ideal conditions for the age of the industrial revolution in the mid-18th century, which arguably is the single most important driver of how we live and work today.

The industrial revolution led to workers, for the first time, being organized en masse rather than in small, artisanal stores. Heightened commercialization showed up across all aspects of the European economy. Ambitious peasants, often through violent means, increased their landholdings with the help of feudal lords, producing large quantities of food for sale in domestic markets.

Domestic manufacturing soared with rural workers working full time to produce thread and cloth under the sponsorship of urban merchants, flush with raw materials from the extractive colonies. Craft work too began to shift in attitude toward a commercial end product.

These changes led to a period of transition in Europe from a heavily bureaucratic, monarch-controlled ruling class to a powerful ownership (capitalist) class and a not so powerful non-ownership (labor) class. This was the birth of classical economic liberalism, characterized by the laissez-faire or free-market capitalism we live in today.

The early industrial revolution was driven by manufacturing and mines—steam engines, iron, coal, and other heavy industries. Led by Britain in the early 1800s, after the chaos of the French Revolution and Napoleonic Wars, Germany, France, and Belgium rapidly industrialized. This set in motion a set of externalities that continuously increased the demand for labor, across all sectors of the economy, new and old.

The scale of industrialization placed higher demands on the ability to transport goods across large distances. This led to massive investments across railroads, canals, and river systems. Created to transport goods, the first commercial rail line for passengers opened between Manchester and Liverpool in 1830.[9] Many Western European nations opened passenger rail lines across the 1830s.

European powers also undertook such projects in extractive colonies to transport resources from the rural areas to the ports. For example, the first passenger railway line in Asia was opened up in Bombay, India, in 1853.[10] In addition to transporting products, railways also gave labor the chance to be somewhat mobile and have some bargaining power within urban areas, even if negligible.

All this led to rapid urbanization, with factory workers needing proximity to factories and power sources. Concentration of labor also allowed new discipline and specialization, which led to constant productivity gains. However, these productivity gains were often driven by horrendous, unregulated working conditions at the factories of the industrial revolution.

Working conditions in factories of the industrial revolution involved unrelenting, repetitive 16-hour workdays, low wages that barely covered the cost of living, and disease-ridden working and living conditions. A laissez-faire approach was adopted by governments and monarchs, laden by the gains through taxation and colonization. This basically meant there were barely any rules in place to protect workers during the industrial revolution.

Some standard practices during the time included the following:

- *Workers were being docked pay for taking a break or having to clean their machines during meals.*

- *Low wages and disparity in wages across men (ten shillings per week), women (five shillings), and children (one shilling). In comparison, families paid five shillings a month in rent and thus had to send their children to work. Child labor was preferred, due to their being significantly cheaper, which meant wages were kept lower, even in times of huge profits.*

- *Lack of safety procedures, leading to injury and death. A report from the British House of Commons in 1832 commented, "There are factories, no means few in number, nor confined to the smaller mills, in which serious accidents are continually occurring, and in which, notwithstanding, dangerous parts of the machinery are allowed to remain unfenced."*[11]

This lack of protection or rights eventually forced workers to organize through unions. While it is a common belief that labor unions were a direct consequence of the works of Karl Marx, the first unions were formed more than a century before, in the mid-18th century. The first recorded labor strike in the US was in 1786 by printers in Philadelphia, who opposed a wage reduction and demanded six dollars a week in wages.[12]

In 1799, the Combination Act was passed,[13] which banned trade unions and collective bargaining by British workers. Although the unions were subject to often severe repression until 1824, they were already widespread in cities such as London.

By the 1810s, the first labor organizations to bring together workers of different occupations were formed. The General Union of Trades may have been the first, founded in 1818 in Manchester. The organization was also called the Philanthropic Society to better protect its true purpose since trade unions back then were illegal.[14]

Workplace militancy had also manifested itself as Luddism, a 19th-century movement in Britain characterized by textile workers destroying machinery, rejecting automation and machines. Workers conducted raids to destroy machinery within textile factories that were perceived to be taking away jobs. It had been prominent in struggles such as the 1820 uprising in Scotland, in which 60,000 workers went on a general strike, which was soon crushed. Sympathy for the plight of the workers brought a repeal of the acts in 1824, although the Combination Act of 1825 severely restricted their activity. This struggle between unions and corporations exists to this day.[15]

The industrial revolution also still affects the modern workforce and the global economy with the shift from an agricultural economy to an industrial one. During the early phases of the industrial revolution, workers across Britain and Western Europe were forced out of peasantry and migrated in large numbers from rural areas into rapidly growing urban industrial centers. Economic textbooks continue to teach students that economic development requires a large-scale transfer of labor from the agricultural/rural sector to more industrialized/ urban sectors of the economy.

This form of economic system almost demonizes agricultural or craft work. And similar mass migrations still take place across the world, from villages to cities, and on a global scale to industrialized countries.

This has happened in India extensively through my lifetime with cities like Mumbai and Delhi adding about 35 million people in a ten-year period between 2012–2022,[16] with their infrastructure literally crumbling under the population's weight. Such levels of migration from villages to cities and to more industrial nations are unsustainable today, something we are seeing play out in election battles across the world.

This being considered the only model of economic development for almost 300 years has meant cities have overflowed across the developed and developing world, extending into their adjoining areas, exploiting their resources. All this while the countryside gets poorer and less livable.

Sadly, some of the horrendous working conditions during the early industrial revolution persist in the now independent, formerly "extractive colonies" across Africa, Asia, and Latin America. We often wake up to headlines of such conditions in the textile factories of India and Bangladesh that fuel global fast fashion, the widespread use of child (Asia and Africa) and bonded labor (Middle East), and the exploitation of workers in the diamond mines of Somalia or cocoa farmers in Ghana. Even in the developed world, we have troubling headlines like these for warehouse workers!

Moreover, the standard nine-to-five workday also comes from the industrial revolution, when workers had to be at their workstations within factories at a particular time, something that should be reasonably irrelevant in today's internet economy.

Shareholder Value Maximization over All Else

In the large corporations that exist today, there is a constant struggle between workers, who want a more equitable distribution of the company's profits, and executives, who enjoy disproportionate rewards while being incentivized to manage a stock price toward shareholder returns over worker needs.

While a company like Google will never openly admit it, experts agree that the 12,000 Googlers who were laid off during the mass tech layoffs beginning in January 2023, despite huge profits and padded balance sheets, were let go to manage the stock price, which is usually a function of margins and earnings.

Alphabet, the parent company of Google, saw its stock lose about 34 percent in value in 2022 from its 2021 level, even as revenues increased during the same period.[17] This meant something needed to be done to stimulate the stock price, as one of the biggest expenses for a company is paying its employees. So, layoffs always directly boost the bottom line.

Layoffs were announced abruptly on January 20, 2023, leading to worker chaos within the company. I knew over 100 people personally who were laid off on the day, some after almost two decades at the company, via an email at about 3 a.m. Friends on maternity and paternity leaves did not know if their parental leaves were going to be paid. Local regulations in different countries meant that the layoffs were immediately impacting 6,000 employees in the US. The other 6,000 around the world would just have to wait to find out over the next few months.

That January, I was on a yearlong assignment in Mumbai from New York, setting up an Asia Pacific and China (APAC) team based in Singapore. My assignment was to end on February 13, 2023, with Google contractually obligated to move me back to the US. However, after losing my boss and the whole organization in America, I learned there was literally no one who had any context on my case, especially with the mass chaos the company was experiencing. I was left to fend for myself, without knowing what would happen to me—whether my layoff would happen in India upending my life completely or whether Google would move me back to the US. Being laid off in India would mean a much lower severance and a whole host of immigration and legal issues to deal with.

Finally, after the most harrowing three weeks of my career, I was able to get Google to move me back to the States, but that was done on a one-day notice! Imagine moving countries on a day's notice!

Additionally, some people who were laid off were being rehired in different roles at Google or being reached out to on LinkedIn by recruiters from Google for similar roles.

But Google achieved its goal: The stock price rose from about $99 to $140 by the end of 2023. In 2024, Google increased operating income by 33 percent, while having an operating margin of 32 percent, effectively making 33 cents on the dollar[18] while continuing to lay off more employees with "silent layoffs" and "voluntary buyouts."

This story was repeated across many tech and non-tech companies through 2023–2024. According to Layoffs.fyi, 1,193 tech companies laid off about 264,000 tech workers globally in 2023, while another 152,000 were laid off in 2024 across 551 companies,[19] all while Nasdaq companies' profits grew at about 20 percent.[20]

This primacy of shareholder value maximization at the expense of workers comes from the 1919 *Dodge v. Ford Motor Co.* case in the Michigan Supreme Court. At the time, Henry Ford wanted to reinvest the considerable retained earnings back into the company, toward research, development, and employee bonuses. The Dodge brothers, though, who were minority investors in Ford, brought a lawsuit against Ford, alleging that his intentions to benefit employees and consumers were at the expense of shareholders. The Michigan Supreme Court agreed, creating the capitalistic principles of today, that shareholder value must be maximized at all costs, via dividends or stock price appreciation or both.

Thus, it is quite clear that companies are not incentivized to reward their employees or consumers over shareholders. That is just how the corporation, as an entity, is incentivized to act.

This is why many executive compensation packages are linked to a company's stock price.

But, as workers, why do we then continue to put up with this? The answer lies in the incentives and the alternatives. Capitalism or the industrial revolution has brought about the most significant gains in collective wealth and standard of living and continues to do so. Whether capitalism continues to generate proportionally collective wealth today is seriously in doubt. Regardless, the capitalistic world governs the experience of "work" for most of us, and working conditions, benefits, and hours have significantly improved in most parts of the world. However, the foundational aspects of what that work is built on remains the same—a lot of labor working for the disproportionate gain of the few capitalists. It was never meant to be for the benefit of the worker, and in a more self-actualized world desiring fulfillment, this creates a recipe for burnout.

Putting Yourself First

Capitalists have always had more bargaining power than labor because the world needs capital in order to make labor productive toward economic activities, and not the other way around. Factory workers were more burned out than any of us can ever begin to imagine; they just did not have any avenues to recover from that burnout.

As a corporate worker today, you should keep all this in mind as you think about your career and its evolution. While you may have the most supportive bosses and teams, your company itself is always incentivized to maximize shareholder value, which is based on unending profits and bottom-line growth.

And while your company may need to market loyalty as a value, it isn't incentivized to be loyal to you. You should not expect loyalty in return. Imbibing cold rationality into your relationship with your company will help your loyalty serve you first. To be clear, there is a difference here between the company, as an entity, and the people you work with. Leaning on the people around you emotionally and feeling a connection are critical, in my opinion, as they are the only people in the world who will truly relate to your daily corporate context.

Evolving your relationship with your corporate job to being more transactional will go a long way toward your not sinking emotionally when something like a layoff happens to you. Stats tell us that it will happen at least once in your career. I had many friends and colleagues who took months to recover from the "way it was done." I didn't need so long to recover and expected it to come, in exactly the way that it did! I didn't expect my company to treat me differently, as I understood the incentives that were driving its behavior, despite its vastly different promises. And I was better off emotionally for it.

This doesn't mean that you shouldn't be passionate about your job or start shirking or hating your company. It just means that you put yourself first, by understanding the principles and incentives that govern a company's existence, making your relationship with your job more rational and transactional than emotional. That will help you feel empowered and approach your job with pragmatism, something that has been baked into the company's approach toward an employee.

CHAPTER 2

Global Capital, Local Labor

If you've ever sat in Economics 101, you know that the foundation of modern capitalism or production rests on four pillars—land, labor, capital, and entrepreneurship. As we learned in the previous chapter, the owners of capital have long had more freedom to find ways of multiplying wealth through existing wealth than labor has had to create wealth with their abilities.

Today, capitalists are incentivized by tax laws to find the best possible returns across the globe through free, global capital markets. Foreign direct investment (FDI) and foreign institutional investment (FII) are capital flows that determine the fortunes of billions of people (labor) all over the world. This mobile or global nature of capital stands in stark contrast to the immobile or local nature of labor.

Workers are bound by location, labor, immigration, and tax laws, often created in consultation with big businesses.

They are also governed by wage rates that are wildly different across countries for the same work, enabling capitalists to profit off global skill-level arbitrage—the basis of outsourcing and global freelancing in the world, which is now slowly being replaced by AI (artificial intelligence), for a steadily higher return on investment.

When workers have experienced mobility, it's typically been in the service of capitalist needs, not their own agency. Agricultural workers were bound to their small farms, until colonists with large farms and plantations needed a global supply of farm labor. Artisans were limited to domestic markets until the capitalists created global art markets to sell their goods at high margins. Soldiers were limited to their barracks until the royals needed them to embark on a conquest. Factory workers were bound to their factories until they were needed at other factories elsewhere. Corporate workers were bound to their jobs until the companies they worked for decided to send them somewhere on projects or relocate them based on "business needs."

This immobility of labor along with a lack of agency, in addition to how hard immigration systems are, creates burnout, at both ends. For example, the average techie in India has a path in mind that takes them to the US or Europe, pining for it, while the average Indian techie in the US is always living in some immigration-related situation. The US immigration system involves well-documented decade-long waits for green cards. The visa structures disincentivize additional employment and mobility as a foreign worker in the US, creating a dependence on the employer, not just as a provider of employment, but also as a provider of the entire context within which you live your life.

I felt this firsthand, when I lost my work visa linked solely to my job at Google in July 2023, which took another 18 months or so to resolve. I was fortunate as my fiancée (now wife) is American. I know friends who have migrated to other countries, only to try to make their way back to the US, to preserve their previous petitions or continue a different status in the country. This immobility and lack of agency bring an emotional tax on immigrants. This is only getting more challenging, as immigrant workers weigh economic progress back home with increasing anti-immigration attitudes in the West.

Labor mobility, while easier as a domestic worker, is still governed by sometimes complex procedures like noncompetes, gardening leaves, notice periods, and so on. You can invest with a swipe of your thumb but can't exit a company as quickly. Thus, there is an emotional tax associated with the immobility of labor relative to the mobility of capital.

The Illusion of Mobile Labor

Only in the last century, and especially after the Second World War, has labor found a higher degree of mobility toward seeking more rewarding, global opportunities. That too has been extremely restricted to what we term "skilled labor" or, in recent decades, educated labor.

The laissez-faire or free-market principles adopted for effective allocation of capital in the world have not been applied to labor at a global scale. This is what leads to the shortages of pub workers in the UK and cleaning staff in the US in a world of Brexit and tariffs when at the scale of the world, we have enough people to easily fill these jobs. If we generally divide the world into two parts—owners of capital and nonowners of capital, based on income and GDP—we would still generally find Western Europe and North America being owners of capital and the rest of the world being owners of labor. This has governed the general direction of capital and labor flows in the new world order since WWII. What was happening through exploitative colonization before was made systemic after WWII.

The rise of countries like India and China in the past two decades might contest the previous statement, but these too are labor-intensive economies with large pools of excess labor that they export to the world, hungry for capital inflows.

I moved across India to Ireland to Singapore to the US, back to India, and then back to the US between 2015 and 2024. As noted earlier, I've seen firsthand the principles, privilege, and processes that govern immigration flows, and how selective they are. In a globalized world, we almost take immigration for granted. While there are multiple short-term paths, long-term immigration systems are designed more to keep people out than to facilitate efficient labor allocation. Thus, an illusion of permanence that drives people to immigrate comes with a real, longer-term emotional cost.

Let's look at India as an example of how this privilege and these principles work. India had 1.4 billion people with a median age of 28.8 years,[1] and 42 percent of graduates under 25 being unemployed in 2023.[2] Its large English-speaking population, high-quality technical education, lower labor wages, and a large domestic market make it an attractive market for the capitalists of the West. In addition, the huge pool of rural and uneducated workers attracts countries in the Gulf that need service workers for their ambitious new cities.

According to India's Ministry of External Affairs, in 2023, there were 32 million non-resident Indians (NRIs) and persons of Indian origin (PIOs) residing outside India, which makes Indians abroad the largest overseas diaspora in the world.[3] Every year, India exports about 2.5 million people overseas, which is the highest annual number of immigrants in the world. India also receives the most remittances, or citizens sending money home while being employed abroad, of any economy in the world: $83 billion in 2020, followed by China ($59.5 billion) and Mexico ($42.8 billion).[4]

In India, trade itself is as old as the Indus Valley civilization itself (2600 BC). Spices, gold, textiles, and many other products were traded, mostly across the subcontinent, Tibet, and Persia. India was known to trade across the Silk Route through towns like Pataliputra, Ujjain, and Puhar as early as 600 BC. Till the Middle Ages, though, India mainly served as a supplier, establishing trade with Persia, the Gulf, and the Far East through the Indian Ocean, which occupies 20 percent of the maritime world.

Indian merchants have been mentioned across Central Asia and Arabia as early as the 16th century. Astrakhan in Southern Russia was where the first Indian merchant colony was established as early as the 1610s.[5] Finance, precious metals, textiles, and indigo formed the basis of these early Muslim, Hindu, and Sikh traders from India and parts of modern-day Pakistan.

The earliest migrations en masse out of India, however, were to Southeast Asia when then emperor Ashoka, who had adopted Buddhism and sought to spread it, invaded Kalinga (modern-day Odisha and Andhra Pradesh) in about 260 BC.[6] The Cholas, who were a powerful dynasty in South India, captured Sumatra

and the Malay Peninsula, leading to "Indianized Hindu" kingdoms being established across modern-day Malaysia, parts of
Indonesia, Cambodia, Myanmar, Laos, Vietnam, and Thailand.
In addition, Indian influence spread across the subcontinent to
areas as far as Tibet, Yunnan (China), and Afghanistan.

The colonial period marked the first major wave of modern migrations out of India, driven by the British needing farm
labor in their colonies in Africa and the West Indies. Indentured
laborers from British India in the mid-19th century were transported to work on plantations in Fiji, East Africa, Malaysia,
Singapore, and the West Indies. These populations evolved to
become entrepreneurs, controlling the diamond and gold trade
in East Africa, for example.

Durban, South Africa, is often considered the largest Indian
city outside India with 1.3 million Indians residing there. Even
Mahatma Gandhi made that journey back in the day, working
as a lawyer in Durban from 1893 to 1896, before he came back
to India and led the freedom struggle.

The system that formed the basis of these mass migrations
was the Indian indentured servitude system instituted by the
British that transported 1.6 million workers to other British
colonies as a substitute to slave labor, which was abolished in
the British Empire in 1833.[7] A similar trend occurred across
other European colonies with most empires abolishing slavery in the 1830s. Each worker had to appear before an officer
designated by the British government of India and declare free
will. The "agreement" was known as *girmit* and these workers
came to be known as *girmityas*.

A girmit from 1912 states that "monthly or daily wages
of men above the age of 15 will be not less than one shilling

and adult females not less than nine pence for every working day."[8] This system was exploitative and was abolished after much furor in 1917.

You could argue the current, steady supply of construction labor from India to the Gulf to build stadiums for the 2022 FIFA World Cup in Qatar or cities in the desert in Saudi Arabia or Dubai has a similar flavor. It is implemented through practices like labor bonds, passports being held for the period of the bond, and crowded housing camps that are a feature of the outskirts of many Middle Eastern cities.

After independence from Britain in 1947, India saw a wave of voluntary, employment-based migration. While the population redistributed after the bloody partition with Pakistan (and modern-day Bangladesh), conservative estimates suggest about 20 million people were displaced and a million dead.[9] My grandparents were among the displaced and my grandfather lost a part of his family too while crossing over to India. Economic hardship, after 200 years of colonial economic drain and a bloody partition, drove people to look for better opportunities, within modern-day India and abroad.

Between 1947 and 1962, there were large migrations from India, primarily Punjab, Haryana, and Bengal, to the UK, following kinship ties. The ability to move unrestricted within the Commonwealth made this an attractive option for Indians in labor-hungry postwar Britain. It was estimated that about 30,000 Indians resided in the UK in 1950, which increased over ten times to 375,000 in 1971.[10]

However, migration volumes changed beginning in 1962 with the passing of the Commonwealth Immigrants Act, which severely restricted the movement of Commonwealth workers into the UK and abolished the provisions of the British Nationality Act of 1948. The Immigration Act of 1971 further controlled migrations to the UK, by means of ancestral linkages to the UK. Still, as of 2020, India remains the largest country of birth for immigrants in the UK,[11] and about 1.8 million Indians reside in the UK today.

The next wave of postindependence migrations out of India was to the Gulf countries, as a result of the region's massive oil extraction and construction boom that began in the 1970s. Retail and construction trades were popular for migrants lacking postsecondary education, while those with higher levels of training went into sectors like health care. Indian nurses and doctors form a large part of medical professionals in the Middle East.

According to India's Ministry of External Affairs, there were about 8.5 million Indians residing across the Gulf states in 2018, with about 5.9 million being in UAE and Saudi Arabia.[12] However, migration from India to the Gulf peaked in 2014 due to a combination of factors. Better prospects back home due to higher rates of education, the ill treatment of blue-collar workers through horrendous working conditions, the raising of work permit–related fees, and the attempts to "nationalize" the workforce through hiring of "locals" were factors. In addition, the inability to naturalize as citizens in Gulf states has led to Indians seeking a better deal, either back home or elsewhere.

The Indian government has also had to answer distress calls for blue-collar workers across the Gulf states, due to situations like company closures. Between 2016 and 2018, it is claimed that the government of India facilitated the involuntary return of a million workers from the Gulf.[13]

Additionally, Kerala, traditionally the state that sent the most blue-collar workers to the Gulf, has seen a large uptick in developmental indicators and is often considered the most livable and developed state in the country. It has the highest literacy rate in India at 96.2 percent with a per capita income of approximately $4,400 per year, almost twice the national average.[14]

Interestingly though, remittances to India from the Gulf have continued to grow, which indicates that more educated Indians residing in these Gulf states earn higher wages, especially across sectors like health care, hospitality, and construction.

Another parallel wave of migrations out of India began in the 1970s to the "New World" of the US and Canada. This is the wave of highly educated Indian doctors, engineers, and finance professionals we see to this day. India has the highest number of postsecondary degree holders abroad, with 3.1 million Indians residing across the 38 countries concentrated in Europe and North America that form the Organization for Economic Co-operation and Development (OECD). The OECD works to stimulate global trade and capitalism. In 2018, China with 2 million and the Philippines with 1.8 million formed one-fifth of the OECD workforce with postsecondary degrees.[15]

This growth has been made possible by the revocation in country-origin quotas that have guided US immigration policies since the 1920s and penalized large nations, like Asian countries and others not from northwest Europe, by design. The introduction in 1990 of H-1B visas for workers in specialty occupations—aimed at attracting highly educated Indians to the US—has accelerated this migration. About 72 percent of the 400,000 H-1B visas issued every year are to highly educated Indians.[16]

While this policy may sound extremely friendly, a little look under the surface, especially at green card or permanent residency policy in the US, reveals a colder, more rational side. I've experienced this firsthand, being on a visa in the US for about five years, while in the process of securing employment-based permanent residency. While country-origin quotas do not apply to the US visa system, they do apply to the issuance of green cards with no one country being able to secure more than 7 percent of the annual 140,000 or so employment-based green cards issued. This means that wait times for applicants from India and China extend into decades, while Europeans in similar roles tend to get green cards in a matter of months, simply because of lower numbers. The system is designed to keep wait times longer for those from larger nations, which makes sense for the stability of the labor market in the US, because the average immigrant will always be cheaper than the average American worker.

The principles are similar for family-based green cards, which means the wait times are longer for employment-based permanent residents who have finally been able to secure a more permanent future to bring over their loved ones.

All of this points to one thing—the foundational principles of immigration control in capital-rich countries have always disproportionately benefited the capitalists, whether that be companies or countries. The system is designed to serve a purpose, using immigration to fill important labor gaps, right when it is needed. Like the engineers from Asia who are the backbone of the global tech industry, largely based in the US. It has made California the fifth-largest economy in the world, with immigrants taking a big reward but being called upon to fill a crucial gap. Filling this gap created the most valuable companies in the history of humanity and generated disproportionate wealth for their owners and the United States as a nation. This story has repeated itself across markets and time, right from the beginning of the industrial revolution. With immigration getting tighter, this trend will accelerate.

This fundamental immobility of labor has meant that immigration, for most immigrants, has often felt like pushing a boulder up a hill, uncertain about when a sudden, larger counterforce from up above will bring the boulder back down, crushing you in the process. While moving abroad guaranteed immigrants a short-term degree of economic prosperity, it also bestowed immigrants with a long-term burden of emotional uncertainty.

The Evolving Opportunity Cost of Immigration

When this emotional burden of immigration is borne in a context of an alternative existence back home not being as raw a deal as it was even a decade ago, it often leads to feelings of extreme unfulfillment, especially in the highly educated class of immigrants. South Asian literature, music, and cinema is rife with such a pining.

Let's explore this thought, which is a constant, relatable tennis match in my own head. The opportunity cost of migrating from developing countries like India and China has risen, especially for the educated class. This can be understood in many ways. Let's look at simple proxies and their relationships to understand the interactional dynamics of capital and labor in a modern economy—increase in company valuations measured by stock market returns and corresponding labor income growth.

Looking at average market indices, growth across both capital-intensive (immigrant inflow) and labor-intensive (emigrant outflow) markets can help us understand the economic value the corporate sector or capital is creating year over year. Or it can tell us whether labor in an economy should directionally be gaining or losing while working for corporations in that market.

Relational dynamics between stock market value, or simply how much companies are collectively worth, and labor income, the portion of those rewards labor reaps, can help us understand who is gaining more proportionally from economic activity. Comparing the US and India from this perspective can give us some insight into this mental trade-off that highly educated immigrants (or corporate workers) are constantly evaluating, since about three in four H-1B visas are granted to Indians.

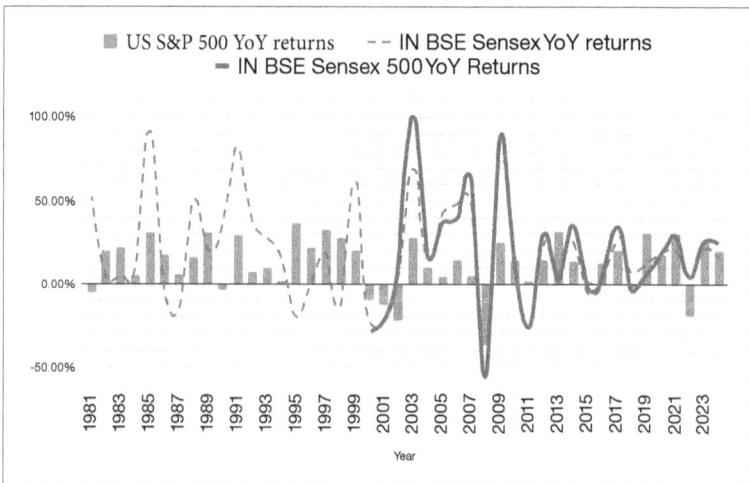

Stock market return comparisons (US vs. India). (Source: NYU Stern, BSE Archives)

The chart presents an oversimplified view of major indices for an immigrant inflow market (US S&P 500) versus an emigrant outflow market (India Bombay Stock Exchange, or IN BSE), which tells us a few things:

- *The strength and depth of the US stock market as an investor is unmatched over the long term.*

- *Due to the base effect, the Indian stock market was prone to wilder swings, but those swings have reduced and become more predictable. In other words, Indian equity markets are beginning to mature. This is generally true for many immigration outflow markets.*

- *The average returns of the top 500 companies by market cap in India in the 2020s are beating the average returns in the US by about a third. Thus, the corporate sector is growing at a much more rapid pace in India. Therefore, relatively speaking, immigration outward is less attractive from the perspective of employment and investment opportunities, even compared to a few years ago.*

Average Index Growth Rates by Decade

Decade	Avg. S&P 500 growth rate	Avg. IN BSE Sensex growth rate	Avg. IN BSE Sensex 500 growth rate (available since 2000)
1980s	18%	24%	
1990s	19%	24%	
2000s	1%	22%	
2010s	14%	10%	10%
2020s	15%	16%	20%
Avg. since 1981	13%	19%	18% (*since 2000)

(Source: NYU Stern, BSE Archives, Motilal Oswal)

Additionally, labor income growth trends, based on UN International Labor Organization (ILO) data, mimic corporate profits more closely in India than they do in the US.[17]

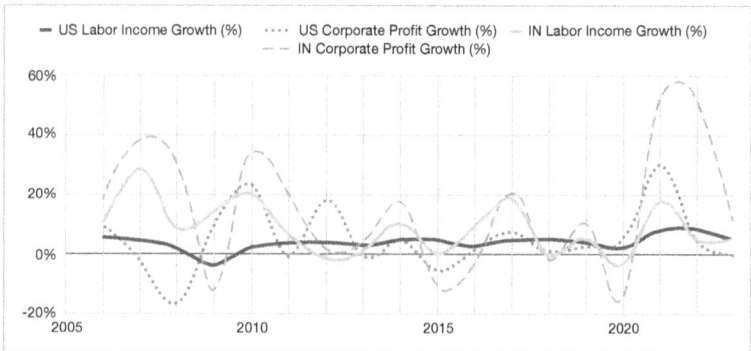

Income and corporate profit growth.
(Source: ILO Data, US Bureau of Economic Analysis)

What this does is create a sense of synergy between key economic agents—corporations and labor pulling together in one direction and having a relatively similar "skin in the game." In the US, the rate of labor income growth year over year has been steady in the low single digits, even as corporate profits increase or decrease.

US vs. India corporate profit / labor income / GDP growth

US			India		
Non-inflation adjusted corporate profit growth (2023 vs. 2005)	Non-inflation adjusted total labor income growth (2023 vs. 2005)	Non-inflation adjusted GDP growth (2023 vs. 2005)	Non-inflation adjusted corporate profit growth (2023 vs. 2005)	Non-inflation adjusted total labor income growth (2023 vs. 2005)	Non-inflation adjusted GDP growth (2023 vs. 2005)
124% (2.2x)	99% (~2x)	110% (2.1x)	819% (9x)	327% (4.3x)	745% (8.4x)

(Source: United Nations ILO data through ILOSTATExplorer | Federal Reserve Bank of St. Louis Economic Data.)

Note: The India Consumer Price Index rose 245 percent in the same period vs. 65 percent for the US.

Simply put, the ratio of labor income growth to general price level growth in India was 1.3 while that in the US was at 1.5, which means labor gained slightly more buying power in the US over the time period. However, this doesn't account for absolute growth and income inequality in the US, benefiting a far smaller proportion of the population.

According to the World Bank, the Gini coefficient (0–100), which measures the level of income inequality in an economy, was 25.5 for India and 41.7 for the US in 2022.[18] Thus, income inequality is much higher in the US and labor income growth alone doesn't tell us the story of the average corporate worker in the US.

When you look at the last ten years and ahead to the next ten years, these trends at this level of economic maturity change things. The Indian economy broke out in the last ten years, doubling, by adding jobs in high-tech, industrial sectors at scale, to grow to a nearly $4 trillion economy through a wave of digitization that catapulted it from a paper-driven economy into a mobile-driven economy, skipping the desktop phase of digitization altogether. By 2035, the Indian economy is expected to grow to 2.5 times its current size, about $10 trillion, while the US economy is projected to grow to 1.4 times its current size or about $40 trillion.[19]

While the Indian economy faces the challenge of achieving broad-based growth for over 1.6 billion people, for a certain section of highly educated labor, prospects have never been better. Thus, both in absolute and relative terms, for highly educated immigrants, the opportunity cost of leaving everything behind is becoming much higher. Additionally, the real cost of an opportunity in the US has also increased for the immigrant, with the increasing cost of education and rising inflation in the US. There are obviously many other factors at play in this decision-making for an immigrant. However, that foundational question that drives immigration has an ever-evolving answer, especially for highly educated Indians (or other countries in a similar growth cycle).

The answer to the existential cost-benefit evaluation of leaving everything behind was much simpler in the past, which made things easier at an emotional level. It has gone from an internal narrative of "I gotta do what is better for me and my family economically" to "Is all this even worth the sacrifice?"

On the other hand, with the slowing rates of income growth, and corporate profits not really affecting general labor income, in addition to the same job requiring more expensive degrees, the corporate sector in turn becomes less attractive to educated workers in the US.

This constant evaluation for many highly educated workers, whether immigrant or not, who form the crux of the corporate world, is a mental petri dish for burnout. Burnout itself manifests from a constant feeling of restlessness, driven by a perceived lack of agency over your own life and the immobile setup of labor in general. As an immigrant, you are also constantly evaluating costs versus benefits of a relatively improving existence back home while continuing to climb up a ladder that you have an eerie feeling will leave you unfulfilled emotionally.

With the awareness that capital drives labor movements, as a burned-out corporate worker, you should evaluate the context of your life that fulfills you the most. Especially as an immigrant, get clarity on why you are choosing or not choosing a path, and prioritize what you desire, unapologetically so. And this could be as simple as wanting home-cooked food or the need for recreational space or wanting to earn a particular currency/wage rate. It just needs to work for your own mental petri dish.

CHAPTER 3

The Education System

Think about a time when you felt stuck or stifled with the options that your professional path presented. Do you remember your general thoughts and emotions at the time? What expectations did you have when you started on that path? Do you wish you could go back and change some choices you made along the way?

I've felt this "stuckness" many times through the various stages of my career as a generalist, evaluating different paths, most recently when I secured permanent residency in the US after a 14-month hiatus of being unable to work in America. I was faced with the choice of taking my career in a different direction or trying to rejoin the corporate path where I left off.

During such ponderings, I've usually been able to break my feelings down into an expectations versus reality equation. While I'm sure that isn't the most insightful thing you've heard, think about why the mismatch between that expectation and reality might have occurred in your own life.

It is because the expectations you had of your path in two, five, ten, or twenty years, and the reality of that path, in terms of your own perception of reward and fulfillment, don't match. Thinking of your life as a predefined path, with milestones and comparisons, makes you constantly ponder over this existential expectation versus reality equation, steeped in arbitrary milestones. The challenge, especially in this modern world obsessed with exceptionalism, is that our paths offer the false promise of infinite possibility and underestimate the reality of finite choices.

The Pressure to Be on a Path

Remember that favorite interview question we've all asked or been asked: *Where do you see yourself in five years?*

Now think about yourself, your industry, or the job you did five years ago. Has all of that changed beyond recognition? The job I did as recently as 2016 is now basically done by a button. Software developers, who commanded the highest-paying jobs till only a few years ago, are being rapidly challenged by AI or scrambling to become AI engineers, reduced to supervisory roles. Subscriptions as a primary business model, for example, was only adopted in the last five years or so. AI wasn't a word in the public consciousness till 2023, and today, we're told we should let it run our lives, from making us breakfast to writing our resumes and picking candidates for jobs!

So, if companies themselves do not know their paths, why is there that pressure on individuals? Based on my own experience, that interview question itself is ill-advised. Someone who is extremely sure of their path, despite knowing how rapidly their context may evolve, is already a bit stifled.

This stifling, myopic path, especially if you're not fulfilled by it, again brings with it a sense of constant jadedness and exhaustion. It is that exhaustion, coupled with a perceived lack of agency over your path, that eventually manifests as full-blown burnout. Being flexible and adaptable, and rebuilding agency over your own skills are key to building long-term careers today, especially in a time when the AI, internet, and gig economy is truly enabling infinite possibilities at an individual level.

While human beings need structure in their lives, society starts laying out that structure for us from the moment we barely attain consciousness, not leaving too much room for exploration. Remember that question of what you wanted to be when you grew up? I'm guilty of asking this question myself to my nine-year-old niece. She insists she wants to be a vet, which is adorable. I think I wanted to be a cricketer back then. Those questions gave me and my niece structure to explore our personalities, but had I stuck to that path, given the context of my life (my state didn't even have a team back then), I probably wouldn't have made a career out of it!

As a 16-year-old, I could have never imagined living in four countries, traveling to over 60 countries, marrying an American woman, and attaining financial independence, all before or around 30 years of age. And I am so glad I had the openness to explore divergent paths while still committing to a fairly traditional corporate path. Metaphorically speaking, I knew that I wanted to sail west in the Atlantic, but I was open to landing in Brazil, Mexico, the US, or Canada. That openness has enabled me to start afresh, after 11 years at Google, through this book, and through a coaching and workplace culture consultancy, WideWorldView.com, while continuing to positively engage with the corporate world.

While predefined paths are great to give our expeditions structure, we still need to adjust our sails as per the direction of the winds and currents. As a society, we are too eager to force-fit people into paths, generally very early in life. Thinking about your life and identity as one thing or one path stifles you from exploring all other potentially more fulfilling identities. Despite the rapid changes in societal structures and expectations, the corporate ladder is still largely not set up for individuals to be able to adjust their sails to changing winds, without making radical shifts in course.

What if these paths that society puts us on and we often unquestioningly follow weren't meant for us at all? What if we followed those paths because we constantly felt a stifling opportunity cost? What if those paths were designed to stifle innovation and exploration at a personal level? And what if the expectations our paths set for us were never based in reality? Who made us feel that these paths were the only ones we had? The answer is largely rooted in our modern education system, which is designed to prioritize "getting a job" over self-discovery.

Foundations of Our Education System

Today, education systems around the world are built to serve a system defined by the fruits of the industrial revolution.

Like most aspects of the lives we live, colonization has had an impact, with education systems across the colonies usually mimicking those of mother countries.

As European colonists became more powerful in the "extractive colonies," Europeanism came to be more in fashion. Everyone aspired to be like their colonizers, and arguably still do. This partly explains the large-scale adoption of Spanish and Portuguese across Latin America, French across North Africa, and of course English across Asia, the British Empire, and most of the world.

Education across the world was intertwined with religious studies, early on in Persia, the Indian subcontinent, China, Japan, parts of Africa, and, much later, Europe. Some of these colonies had well-established education centers that focused both on the spiritual and scientific aspects of learning mixed with religious studies.

The first schools were established under the Xia dynasty in 2000 BC in China. The University of al-Qarawiyyin located in Fes, Morocco, is the oldest existing, continually operating,[1] and the first-degree-awarding educational institution in the world, according to UNESCO and Guinness World Records. The Nalanda University established in fifth-century Bihar, India,[2] is also one of the oldest-running universities in the world and was the center of Vedic mathematics, the field that gave us the number zero and many other mathematical equations introduced to the world through European names, like the Fibonacci sequence.

In most of the Western world though, education was mostly private and at home till the Middle Ages. Early European universities, like the University of Paris, established in 1160,[3] had a basis in Christianity, just as their Asian counterparts had basis in religion more than a thousand years earlier. By the 18th century, universities across Europe started publishing academic journals. By the 19th century, elementary education in reading, writing, and arithmetic was being provided in Western, Central, and parts of Eastern Europe mostly because politicians believed that education was necessary for orderly political behavior.

The European education system that forms the basis of most education systems across the world today traces back to the principles these universities established in post-Renaissance Europe.

European colonization brought Christian missionaries to the colonies, all of whom set up educational institutions that, endorsed by the colonizers, became attractive to the locals. There were also cultural elements to this, with a majority of locals being keen to adapt to the demands of a new perceivably "superior" world order.

I went to St. Edmund's School, Shillong, an Irish Catholic school that runs 30-plus schools and colleges across India, followed by St. Xavier's College, Mumbai, run by Roman Jesuits. Both were established over 100 years ago. I grew up around a school chapel that stood as the oldest brick structure in my town, studying the same curriculum as the General Certificate of Secondary Education (GCSE) in the UK. Europeans brought with them the might of their technology, fueled by the industrial revolution, and overawed the locals. Despite the ill treatment, many locals in the colonies believed that the systems of their colonizers were better and wanted to adopt them, something I saw growing up every day, even in the 1990s.

In India for example, education, specifically a European/English education, was (still is) perceived to be an escape for millions from extreme poverty, defined generationally by the caste system. About 70 percent of the country is still considered "lower caste," and sadly the perils associated with the caste system still play a role in parts of Indian society. In addition to the caste system, during the 1800s and 1900s, the zamindari, or the feudal system, ensured that most of the populace had no shot at a better life.

When locals around the colonies saw prospects of factory work that the industrial revolution brought in mother countries, it was perceived as a better deal and a better life. Thus, that Westernized education seemed like the only shot at a better path, something that holds true to this day.

So, what should education strive to achieve for an individual and the collective?

In 1918, Perley G. Nutting, an American physicist, wrote in his journal article "The Principles of Education" that "education covers the span of our lives, from the cradle to the grave. . . . During school days, the mind receives and assimilates ideas from further afield not associated with desire or comfort. Later on, in high school and college days, the mind likes and readily assimilates groups of abstract related ideas and even probes the infinite and unknowable. In middle life, the dominant interest lies in the practical problems of everyday life. In later life, after the details of most minor problems have become familiar, interest turns once more to general principles and larger problems. In short, education is as long and broad as our lives."[4]

While this is a more principled and, in my opinion, truer assessment of the purpose of education and how everyone should perceive it, today, education is thought to be for the purpose of practical, gainful employability.

He goes on to say, "In our present system of education, the responsibility of the nation to the individual is recognized for that part of the individual's mental education that he receives from textbooks. No attempt is made to instruct him or even to supervise his instructions in later life."[5]

Education Today

More than 100 years on, not much has truly changed. Personal experience for most of us shows a similar lack of practicality that education imparts on the individual, with focus being more on accumulation of knowledge rather than helping the individual process information overload along with a focus on physical, emotional, financial, and moral education.

Society continues to use expensive, often impractical higher education to signal worth to the labor market. While the internet has democratized learning and access to work in many ways, it is yet to truly change how it affects conventional large-scale employability, especially at the very early stages of an individual's career.

In addition to colonization and the systems it brought, another important milestone in the development of modern education systems occurred in the US in the early 1900s with the formation of the General Education Board. On January 15, 1902, a small group of influential men gathered at the home of banker Morris K. Jessup to discuss education. Among the many influential men was John D. Rockefeller Jr. That day, the discussion focused on raising education standards and widening educational opportunities.

A second meeting was held on February 27, 1902, at Rockefeller Jr.'s home. At the end of that meeting, it was announced that Rockefeller Sr. would donate $10 million for the inauguration of an educational program, which created the General Education Board. It was incorporated by an act of Congress on January 12, 1903, with the noble objective of "promoting education within the United States, without the distinction of race, sex or creed."[6]

Eventually, Rockefeller Sr. would give $180 million to the program, which was primarily put toward higher education and medical schools in the US along with improving farming standards in the southern US. The board continued its activities till 1960, making extremely important contributions to expand access to education, especially for African Americans across the South. In 1960, its responsibilities were subsumed by the Rockefeller Foundation. This also helped make education a vehicle for African American empowerment in the US.

While the board's contributions were important in terms of access, it also had a focus on changing education toward industrial skills, thus focusing on generating a pipeline of qualified workers for American corporations. Two areas of emphasis were demonstrative farming and industrial education. This, essentially, was the beginning of vocational training and specialism becoming the foundation of higher education.

A 1992 paper by Louise E. Fleming and Rita S. Saslaw titled

"Rockefeller and General Education Board Influences on Vocationalism in Education, 1880–1925" delves into some of the outcomes of this approach.

The paper defines vocationalism as "generally regarded as the basic purpose for education. It does not refer to offering supplemental manual courses, but it refers to the substitution of education for its own sake, for education for future roles in the job market."[7]

As a principle, before this, education wasn't generally thought of as a path to a job. With the industrial revolution and the increasing power of businesses and business leaders in the new world order, this began to change.

The paper also states, "This change in what schools were expected to do was brought about by many factors. The changing student populace was a major factor, as more and more children filled and overfilled classrooms and as more and more of the children came from poor families, many of them immigrants. Therefore, some changes occurred as a result of the humanitarian impulse, as people and organizations sought to make education understandable and meaningful. However, not all of the people advocating changes had the interests of the children in their hearts. It will be seen that some business people systematically and deliberately acted to stimulate vocationalism in schools, particularly for children who were rural or poor.

"As the story unfolds it is evident that Rockefeller believed that the best education for poor youth was vocational, presumably so that they would be able to maintain occupational positions in their adult lives. The difficulty with philanthropy directed toward vocational programs is that although, in the eyes of the benefactors, the young people were being given a chance, that chance was severely limited to whatever training program the students took."[8]

JP Morgan was another important contributor to such programs, with both Rockefeller and JP Morgan chipping in to establish the New York School of Design, for example. Other prominent institutions established or benefited included Pratt Institute in Brooklyn, and The Wilson Industrial School. Rockefeller also served on the board of many educational institutions and industrial education bodies, actively contributing to the direction of curriculum across the country.

It is quite clear that Rockefeller and the most powerful businessmen in the US, through their actions, indicated a keen and continuing interest in providing vocational and industrial training to people who were to go on to do factory and manual work. Many of these were from poor, immigrant families without an ability to make a living in other ways. Therefore, many philanthropists obviously endorsed these efforts.

Nobody can argue against the fact that the general economic effect vocational education has had on the masses is positive. However, it also served a similar purpose as blinders on a racehorse at an individual level. Paths became much more linear, with an illusion of clarity and infinite choice. Go to school, get a vocational degree, get to work, and be thankful for the life it afforded you. While this approach to education opened doors for a large section of the marginalized population (and still does), it doesn't account for the mental doors it closed, at a personal level, to other aspects of life a student potentially wished to pursue. These linear paths limit people from acquiring diverse skills at an individual level.

This led to a degradation of the reputation of a liberal arts education with a clear shift toward vocational education in the early 1900s, in what came to be termed as the Progressive Era. Technical or specialist or vocational education with the prospects it provided in industry began and continues to be looked at more favorably, leading to a belief that only people who are "good for nothing" take up subjects like literature, philosophy, or history.

As an Indian who studied economics, I have seen this obsession firsthand. Indian families have traditionally been obsessed with two paths that are perceived to be karmic, an escape from poverty toward a better life—an engineer or a doctor. Quality technical and medical education is highly sought after and extremely difficult to achieve in the country.

The IIT-JEE (Indian Institute of Technology Joint Entrance Examination) exam attracts over a million aspirants every year for about 18,000 seats across 23 Indian Institutes of Technology (IIT) across India. In 2023, over 1.1 million aspirants sought 17,385 seats.[9] This system, which rewards less than 2 percent of the aspirants, also generates big coaching businesses in India, with students who make it often guaranteed high-paying corporate jobs. Some names that have come out of IITs are the likes of Sundar Pichai (Google) and Narayana Murthy (Infosys), to name a couple.

This obsession then repeats across many tiers of technical engineering colleges and entrance tests in India, with seats through donations also being a standard practice at many lower tiers of colleges. It creates a cycle of bargaining, trying to stick to a path you chose to commit to at 14, which might be a suboptimal choice for your aptitudes.

It has also created interesting outcomes with entire towns like Kota in Rajasthan popping up as "coaching towns" for millions of students as young as 14, moving from all over the country to focus on the IIT-JEE exam.

A similar hysteria is repeated at a postgraduate level with the Common Admissions Test, a GMAT-like exam that sees over 300,000 aspirants vie for about 5,000 seats across 21 Indian Institutes of Management (IIMs). I too was one of 300,000 students back in 2012, making it to IIM Shillong, but eventually choosing to join Google at an entry-level job, something that absolutely shocked my family. I, after all, was refusing the Indian dream, which has traditionally been characterized by an IIT followed by an IIM education.

Thus, modern education systems with a focus on vocational education have created an environment where liberal arts and academia are generally frowned upon and not well paid. This disincentivizes interest-based education toward prospect-, path-based education.

The Modern "Stuckness" of These Paths

That sinking feeling of not having followed your heart manifests much later, deep into people's careers, as they feel trapped in a life that might have fulfillment in terms of material comforts but lacks emotional fulfillment. Without the material comforts, the path becomes even harder to digest. Most of us are searching for a career that provides a comfortable life as per material definitions of today's world, which we are mistakenly told will also provide us with a life of emotional fulfillment.

However, after attaining a certain standard of living, by solving basic physiological and safety needs, humans strive for fulfillment and self-actualization, eager to serve a higher purpose as illustrated by Maslow's hierarchy of needs.

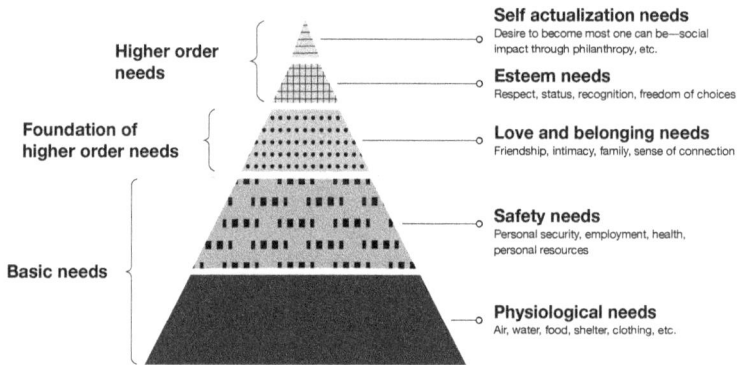

Maslow's now-popular concept of the "hierarchy of needs" first appeared in his 1943 paper "A Theory of Human Motivation" published in *Psychology Review.*

And, what happens when most of the world has achieved these basic needs? This is what we are seeing playing out in the West, especially the US, with most basic needs met as compared to the developing world, yet with people reporting the highest rates of burnout, unhappiness, and loneliness in the world.

The slower economic growth in the West, along with rising costs of education, housing, and living, have led to a decline in prospects for college graduates. An outcome of the rise of vocationalism and necessity of higher education has been the exponential rise of student debt. Looking at education through the lens of return on investment, taking on student debt, especially for higher education, has become the norm.

According to the National Center for Education Statistics (NCES), the total cost of attaining a degree at a public four-year institution in the US increased 84 percent[10] between 2000 and 2022 while median household income increased 15.7 percent![11] According to *Forbes,* student debt stood at $1.75 trillion in 2023. On average, $28,950 is owed per borrower, and 55 percent of students from public four-year institutions took on student loans, with 43 million people in the US currently carrying student debt, or more than 10 percent of the total population.[12]

You would think this is a young people problem. However, as shown in the following chart, the largest bearers of this debt are 35–49-year-olds, with $622 billion or around 39 percent. People are also carrying this debt well into their 50s and 60s, with people over 50 accounting for approximately 24 percent of this debt.

Amount owed in Federal Student debt (USD) - 2023

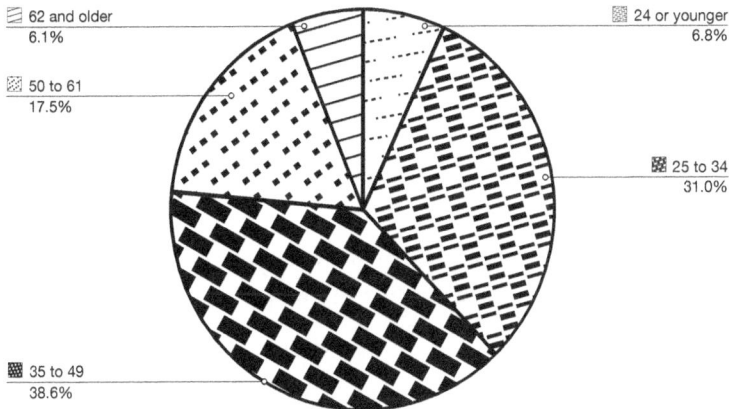

62 and older 6.1%	24 or younger 6.8%
50 to 61 17.5%	25 to 34 31.0%
35 to 49 38.6%	

(Source: *Forbes,* "Student Loan Debt Statistics: Average Student Loan Debt," April 18, 2024)

Thus, this system is making people work harder for longer to just be able to pay back their education loans, and it is even affecting retirement ages, with the US average retirement age jumping from 57 in 1991[13] to 62 in 2024.[14] Moreover, according to a 2022 Gallup survey, people working expect to retire at 66.[15] Additionally, parents are having to save up for children's college funds, lowering their own standard of living.

The National Association of Colleges and Employers has published the *Salary Survey* report since 1960 and tracks starter salaries for college graduates across 110 different disciplines in the US, presenting a window into the declining returns from these loans too. In 1993, the average starter salary for college graduates with a bachelor's degree in the US was $28,080 per year. This rose to about $62,000 per year in 2022.[16] The 30-year rise in salaries barely covers for the 3 percent or so average annual rate of inflation!

Meanwhile, the median house price in the US went from $127,000 in 1993 to $423,000 in 2023, a 3.3 times increase.[17] So, not accounting for inflation and the much higher cost of attaining the same education, graduate salaries were up 2.2 times as compared to the 3.3 times increase in median house prices. This existential challenge has only gotten worse for Americans in the last decade or so, with the median house price doubling from $221,100 in Q4 2012 to $442,600 in Q4 2022! And this trend is even worse in urban centers, where there is more demand for college-educated workers. This creates a vicious cycle of diminishing rewards for educated workers, where inflation, education, and living costs are locking people in for decades.

Moreover, even a starter job, and this declining purchasing

power, is becoming harder and harder to secure after college, bringing into question this entire economic path. According to Oxford Economics, for the first time since 1980, college graduates in 2025 have a higher unemployment rate than the national average in the US, 6 percent versus 4.2 percent! The unemployment rate for this demographic (22- to 27-year-olds) has jumped 85 percent since 2023.[18]

Thus, our education system today is designed to push a predefined path to apparent prosperity with an emphasis on vocationalism, with the end goal being an industrial output as a job. For a long time, that path did afford you an enviable standard of living, especially in the West.

That path that has been sold to most of us had an inherent acceptance that making more money than previous generations of your family should make you more fulfilled. The nobility of being able to provide for your family was marketed hard and was confused with self-fulfillment. However, we ended up creating a society that fulfills material needs over emotional ones.

That perceived return on investment has declined significantly with college graduate salaries in the US barely deemed livable. This has meant more people take on expensive post-graduate degrees to signal capability to the labor market and end up, in a way, even more enslaved to corporate paths that must be financially rewarding for longer, to pay back steep student loans. That's an experience that is so common in my own professional circle. What's more, even if you go bankrupt, student loans are almost impossible to write off in the US. So, it really is your debt for life.

While this problem is stark in the US and UK, Asian economies are at an early stage in a similar cycle that will play out over the next few decades, especially in relation to high-paying postgraduate degrees. Even with rising education costs, this problem isn't realized in developing nations as the return on investment for education is still relatively high, like it was in the 1970s, '80s, and '90s in the US. Moreover, there is still global demand for highly technical skills.

This education system and path did lift billions out of poverty and continues to do so, but it also helped owners of capital garner disproportionate wealth as compared to the labor they employed. This trend is only getting worse with increasing inequality everywhere in the world. This system was never solving for the fulfillment of the individual industrial or factory worker, or even of the CEO for that matter.

More Education for More Work

It seems reasonable to think that more education, and the accompanied higher debt, would mean better, fulfilling jobs. However, especially in the West, with slowing economies and rising inflation, higher and higher education is now needed to get similar entry-level jobs, which are often unfulfilling and are starting to feel like an extremely raw deal, creating a large expectation versus reality mismatch.

I was interested in uncovering whether higher rates of education lead to lower rates of long working hours, and thus lower rates of burnout, and if this differed by country and region. A 2019 study by Savvy Sleep (formerly Sleep Junkie) that looked at burnout rates across 69 cities in 53 countries indicated that Western Europe has the lowest rates of burnout, with Asia having the highest.

Tokyo ranked as the most burned-out city in the world, followed by Mumbai, a city close to my heart and one that framed me. Long commutes and work hours there are just an accepted norm. Workers in Mumbai, according to the study, worked an average of 3,314 hours annually, 1.7 times higher than the global average of 1,985 hours, which indicates that longer working hours have a direct link to burnout rates.[19]

In further exploring this connection between long working hours and burnout, I added education to the mix through the International Labor Organization's (ILO) global labor force survey and its handy stat explorer. It is by far the most comprehensive database on labor statistics across the globe. The 2021 survey has data from about 24 million workers across 125 countries with cuts for work hours, education levels, sex, and so on.

It has defined five categories of education for standardization across the world: less than basic, basic, intermediate, advanced, and level not stated. A pre-primary education is less than basic, primary and lower secondary education are basic, upper-secondary and postsecondary non-tertiary education are intermediate, and anything ranging from short-cycle tertiary education to a doctoral degree is advanced.

I looked at ILO's labor force survey to understand how many hours people are working relative to their levels of education on a global level versus India, the US, and France (as EU proxy). Here's what I found:

% of workers working over 40 hours a week

⊞ Less than basic □ Basic ⧄ Intermediate ▦ Advanced

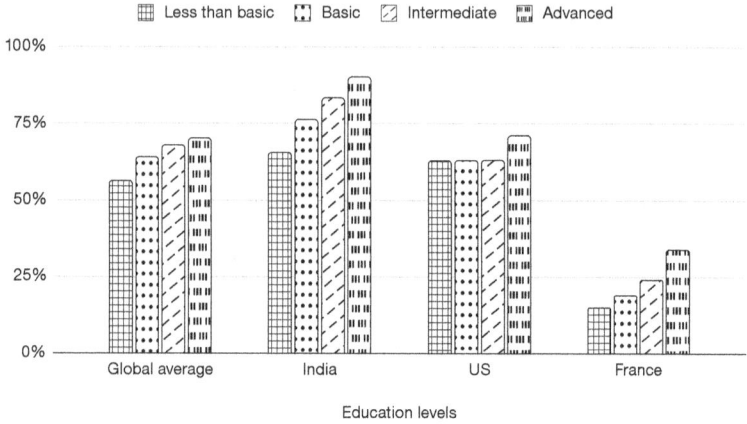

Education levels

(Source: United Nations ILO labor force survey data, 2021)

- *What's clear from the graph is that people with advanced levels of education are working more globally, with each level of education bringing a higher volume of work. Thus, higher education comes with longer working hours.*

- *In India, the situation seems dire, with a significant percentage of all levels of education working over 40 hours, and way above the global averages. About 90 percent of people in India work 40-plus hours a week.*

- *In the US, there seems to be more rigidity in the workday, with no change in the number of hours worked across less than basic, basic, and intermediate levels of education, and people with advanced levels of education working more hours. Also, the percentage of people working over 40 hours in the US is in line with global averages.*

- *France is about a third of the global averages across all levels of education, with just 34 percent of the workers with advanced degrees working 40-plus hours a week as compared to 90 percent in India and 71 percent in the US.*

If we break this down further to look at the percentage of workers working 30–39 hours a week (normal workweek) and those working 49-plus hours a week (long workweek), some starker trends appear.

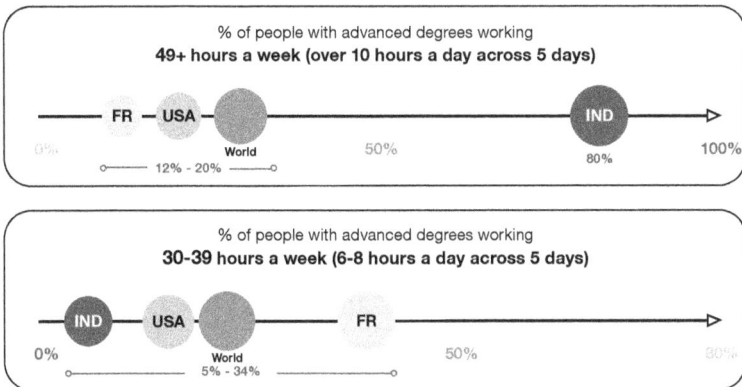

% of people with advanced degrees working
49+ hours a week (over 10 hours a day across 5 days)

FR — USA — World — IND
0%   12% - 20%   50%   80%   100%

% of people with advanced degrees working
30-39 hours a week (6-8 hours a day across 5 days)

IND — USA — World — FR
0%   5% - 34%   50%   80%

(Source: United Nations ILO labor force survey data, 2021)

- *About 80 percent of workers in India with advanced levels of education are working over ten hours a day or 49-plus hours a week, with only 5 percent of workers with advanced degrees having a normal workweek of between six to eight hours a day or 30–39 hours a week.*
- *In the US, 16 percent of the workers with advanced education levels work 49-plus hours a week and only*

12 percent of the workers have a normal workweek of
six to eight hours a day or 30–39 hours a week.

- *In France, only 12 percent of workers with advanced*
  education levels work 49-plus hours a week and 34
  percent have a normal workweek of six to eight hours a
  day or 30–39 hours a week.

Thus, by this data it is clear that France and other EU nations, which show very similar trends, rank well below the global averages (approximately 0.5 times lower) for punishingly long workweeks and well above (approximately 2.5 times higher) the global averages for normal workweeks.

In India, and most other Asian countries showing similar trends, workers with advanced degrees rank well above global averages (about four times higher) for punishingly long workweeks and well below (about 0.6 times lower) the global averages for normal workweeks.

In the US, workers with advanced degrees rank marginally below the global averages for both long workweeks and for normal workweeks (about 0.2 times lower). However, 54 percent of American workers with advanced degrees work 40–48 hours a week, well above the 22 percent in France and the 50 percent global average. This indicates workweeks in the US are generally 20 percent longer than those in France.

Thus, more and more people trying to attain fulfilling lives through higher education end up with longer working hours, especially in Asia. Now this doesn't mean everyone working long hours is burned out and that no one does it out of choice or passion. People with advanced degrees tend to be more employable and in jobs that they probably enjoy, thus working more. But add to this the increasingly higher cost of advanced education, and it is natural for it to feel like a raw deal for many people, driving higher burnout rates.

As a corporate worker or a worker in the world generally, you should find this awareness helpful in understanding how your education, which is extremely important and empowering, has put you on your path that was used and, at times, misused by industry. The implication that industry leaders who commit to philanthropy through education were looking for a more capable workforce for industry is natural and necessary. So, there is no suggestion that there were sinister motives at play. However, the incentives in our systems, endorsed by governments, led us to such a crystallization of paths, lacking individual subjectivity or objectivity.

With that awareness, I encourage you to look back at the education you pursued and ponder the other paths you could have traversed. Did your education truly enable your truest path as a human being, not just as an economic agent?

Today, the return on investment for higher education, measured by both the money you make and the hours you put in, is decreasing. This wasn't true in the '70s, '80s, or '90s, even. Thus, more and more people are naturally feeling burned out and trapped in their ordained paths, which aren't as rewarding as they used to be, especially in the West. What happens when more and more people seeking higher levels of fulfillment are essentially calling this bluff?

**DEFINE YOUR
CAREER IKIGAI**

**MAKE YOUR VALUES
YOUR ANCHOR**

REST STOP ↗

Define Your Career Ikigai

We get on the burnout highway very early in life, and finding perspective while moving at high speed is hard. It is only deep into our careers, after our reality didn't meet the expectations of our early careers, do most of us even start looking for perspective. With the context of how forces of the industrial revolution, the nature of capital and labor, and the path-based education system framed your life, you can now reframe your own journey.

The important thing to understand is that a job or profession does not have to be your identity, but it can and should be a means. You could be taking up a job simply because it pays well, or it is the natural path for your education, or it has flexible working hours, or the boss is nice, or it has the perks you want. As discussed earlier, society and our education system force us to think of work as linear, something that is constant and fixed, linked to identity and something that should be aligned with your passions. Baked into our psyche is the pressure of "what do you want to be when you grow up?"

In truth, it is normal for your work and your own relationship with it to evolve as you and your needs evolve.

While finding work that engages you is critical, being clear about the personal reason behind why you're doing it, which can evolve, will help you anchor when faced with difficult moments. To get to your *why,* there are a few questions that are important to consider and get clarity on—questions that our necessities and a sense of comfort in jobs usually help us shirk.

Explore these questions with curiosity, not judgment, and write your answers down:

- *What drives me as a person?*
- *Why am I doing this job/profession? What are my primary motivators to continue?*
- *What are my day-to-day expectations from my work?*
- *What are the aspects that make me happy?*
- *What are the aspects that make me unhappy?*
- *What are the non-negotiables for me, for current and future work?*
- *If money were not a consideration, what would I want to do? What truly fulfills me?*
- *If I were to take that path, what would my life look like five years from now?*

A framework to help break down the answers to your questions in a more structured fashion is the Japanese concept of *ikigai,* which relates to finding a sense of meaning or purpose in everything you do. In their book *Ikigai,* Hector Garcia and Francesc Miralles have adapted the concept to work and career planning.

Find your ikigai

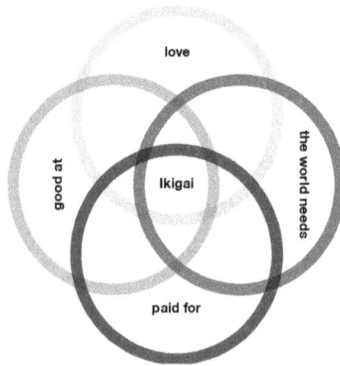

(Source: Hector Garcia and Francesc Miralles, trans. Heather Cleary, *Ikigai: The Japanese Secret to a Long and Happy Life* [Penguin, 2017])

Thinking through this framework will truly help you understand your work and, more importantly, where you can realistically take it. Continuously evaluating your relationship with work or your career ikigai will help you pivot and anchor, in your own needs and not a predefined path. It will allow you to be at peace with why you're currently doing what you're doing and give you clarity on where you want to go next. I've used this framework many times through my corporate career, but it helped me the most after the layoff.

My own career ikigai gave me clarity and focus through the many projects I was trying to work through. After my layoff from Google in July 2023, I suddenly had all this time to work on the many things I pined for. I had at least a year before my permanent residency in the US would come through. I was deep into that process already and the uncertainty of it meant that it didn't really make sense for me to apply for jobs elsewhere—to continue traversing the predefined path I was on. My intention of taking a sabbatical and circumstance had a joyous accident.

I was always into photography, had written an unpublished book in college, was an avid blogger, wanted to do something in the travel industry, and generally had an entrepreneurial mindset. After taking a little break, a few months into my sabbatical, I was open to everything, and I had given all this somewhat of a shot.

Funnily, my sabbatical then started to overwhelm me. I was simply trying out too many hobbies in the hope of making it a career. I started an online photo store, began writing this book, dabbled in freelance consulting, helped my wife start a travel business, and traveled a lot. More importantly, I was trying to do too much too aimlessly—I did not yet have a North Star or mission. I didn't need it at that moment, as being in an open state was necessary for me at the time. However, soon, I felt a need to narrow down my focus. That's when this framework really helped me.

I've always enjoyed finding insight in the mundane, uncovering patterns that seemed obvious to me but were completely revolutionary to others. I built a career off that and the more I thought about it, the more it aligned with my foundational driver as a person. I've always wanted to understand the world and our experiences better, to help me and others around me make sense of invisible strings running our lives. I zeroed in on wanting to help people build emotionally sustainable careers through context-based insights—social, personal, and economic. Once I had that nailed down as a mission, it became easier to find focus, and, more importantly, a common thread running through my work.

I could then easily break down what I wanted to do professionally, and how I could use some of my passions within that.

For example, I've always been fascinated by photography and have the skills to be a travel photographer. However, I thought through all the other things a photographer's job demands, and breaking it down as a passion that could feed into Mountains and Mahals (the travel brand my wife started) saved me from hundreds of hours of work to build a website, do all the marketing required, and buy additional equipment to even begin work as a professional photographer. Through MountainsAndMahals.com, I found a productive, efficient avenue for my passion (photography and writing) to feed into a profession, without making my passion my profession.

This is what my ikigai exercise looked like:

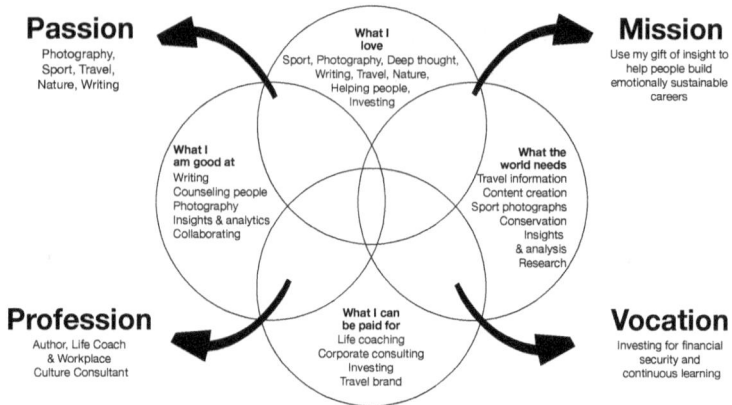

Passion
Photography,
Sport, Travel,
Nature, Writing

What I love
Sport, Photography, Deep thought,
Writing, Travel, Nature,
Helping people,
Investing

Mission
Use my gift of insight to
help people build
emotionally sustainable
careers

What I am good at
Writing
Counseling people
Photography
Insights & analytics
Collaborating

What the world needs
Travel information
Content creation
Sport photographs
Conservation
Insights
& analysis
Research

Profession
Author, Life Coach
& Workplace
Culture Consultant

What I can be paid for
Life coaching
Corporate consulting
Investing
Travel brand

Vocation
Investing for financial
security and
continuous learning

The point of this exercise is not to make you feel like you're giving up on a passion as a profession. What you're doing is structuring what a hobby is versus a profession. You should absolutely find ways to engage with things you love—this will help you break down what could realistically be made a career versus what is a side hustle or just something that helps you relax. This clarity is a powerful thing, especially amid a career transition.

Make Your Values Your Anchor

The ordained paths we accept as gospel early on in our lives and careers disincentivize clarity around personal values and beliefs. Society encourages you to borrow intergenerational values that predefined paths incentivize. While that may work for some, in an increasingly nonformulaic world, an awareness of the values that matter to you need to be your anchor.

The narratives we form of ourselves and of happenings in our lives are the most powerful drivers of how we end up feeling in the day-to-day. Your perception of an experience might be completely different from someone else with the same experience. The perception of circumstances also changes, and your idea of you evolves. That is why any form of true healing requires an evolution of perspective, to one that empowers the current version of you, and not one that beats you down to a pulp.

In a way, we all have a background score to our lives that we have going in our head, a score that frames our perception of the movie that is our life. The writer, director, and main lead of the movie is you and your perception. There is a field of psychology called narrative psychology that focuses on shifting one's perspective and, thus, narratives about life and situations to bring about a more positive outlook and change in individuals.

First developed in the 1970s, narrative psychology was introduced by Theodore Sarbin in the 1986 book *Narrative Psychology: The Storied Nature of Human Conduct*. The internal stories we tell ourselves are critical in framing our realities. It is how we articulate life experiences in a meaningful way, toward a bigger picture, beyond the moment itself.

Stories help us break down our experiences, organize our thoughts, help us find meaning, and, most importantly, frame our anchor to an identity, in an often confusing and lonely world.

Just the awareness that your own mental narrative is driving your life is powerful, as we often ignore that. We ignore it because many of us perceive our realities as somewhat fixed, unquestionable. For example, I am Indian, and in a way that is fixed and unquestionable. However, as my life has evolved to a more international context, living abroad for over a decade and having an American wife, is it really? Does it really matter if I don't feel as "Indian" as I used to before? Narrative psychology essentially focuses on what *your story is and how it has evolved*. And it is okay if your current narrative doesn't align with what you thought was fixed, for your whole life!

Take a minute and think about your own story or narrative. Assess whether the story in your head is generally negative or positive. Now think about your story in terms of your work. What is the narrative there? If the narrative of your life is positive, it is likely you have a more balanced or positive view of things at work too.

Narrative therapy focuses on this question, with a view to finding opportunities for growth and meaning in your story, making breakthroughs through the forging of a new narrative. It enables an externalization of your experiences with an empathetic view of yourself. It gives you almost an outsider's perspective to your own life. This helps individuals quiet the inner critic, with a new understanding of the past and thus help forge a new present and future.

The narrative around mental health in the last two decades has changed from one of chronic illness and shame to recovery and empowerment. Hasn't that helped the world feel more empowered to tackle mental health challenges?

These narratives are also easily built in the corporate world as there are clear, yet arbitrarily defined metrics to form your narrative. Promotions and levels and the money you make are in theory meant to be objective, but in truth, they are extremely subjective and based on the perception of your seniors and colleagues. While there are checks and balances that HR systems try to force into those decisions, eventually it is humans who make those decisions. So, more than your work, vertical growth usually ends up being a perception-driven exercise.

It is easy to form a narrative, either positive or negative, or one of being unfulfilled, based on vertical growth in the corporate world. Additionally, we tend to measure success and failure in relative terms, by comparing ourselves to our peers. This is a dangerous mix as it often ends up with us basing our self-worth on perception-driven realities, of people with misaligned incentives and goals.

Values Audit

My career was successful by every metric. I was "crushing it" in the corporate sense of the term, with roles I held being the envy of many, even within Google. I was promoted five times in the first nine years at Google, traveled to over 30 countries for work, was one of the youngest people managers in the entire business organization, and so on. I was moving on up, with ever more responsibility, and I had an expectation of feeling fulfilled by it. But I wasn't, and my internal narrative continued to be one of shame, of not having lived up to my inner values, in the truest sense of the word.

It was a narrative of someone who felt like an impostor, who somehow felt that he didn't deserve the opportunities he got. I pined over the missed opportunities of building a career based on my passions, and how fulfilled that path would have made me feel, without much knowledge of what that path would have entailed. It was a pointlessly disempowering, draining narrative, and that was my perception of my truth at the time.

That narrative was linked to the expectations I had of my career and my alternate career options. It was also built upon expectations of fulfillment from jobs after various promotions, something that the corporate machinery fed me, and I lapped up.

My expectations, or what you can call my expected narrative about work, as I was growing up, were all-consuming. I believed that I would work on something I was extremely passionate about, not driven by money but by positive social impact. Thus, I expected my work to give my life meaning as that is what I had learned to seek from elders around me. I also expected it to align effortlessly with my values. In truth, most careers are built through a combination of pragmatism and using an internal narrative to match parts of your passion, values, and drive to your work.

About nine years in, after moving through four offices on three continents and six roles at Google, chasing that deep meaning in my work, I felt exhausted and unfulfilled. That was when I took a nonjudgmental view of my life and all that I had accomplished to reevaluate the narrative that was driving my life. My therapist constantly talked down my harsh inner voice and asked me if someone would stay my friend if I spoke as harshly about them. I got to a point where I needed to understand if the punishment I was putting myself through fit my crime.

I forced myself to think through my story from the perspective of other people in my life. I put myself in the shoes of various people in my life and looked at my own life through their eyes. I even asked a few good friends and colleagues what they thought about my life and its design—what they perceived as good or bad.

This helped me externalize my narrative and contextualize it through the bigger picture of my life—where I came from, where I had gotten to, and how someone else would tell my story. That bigger picture is hard for most of us to acknowledge as we are all caught in the weeds of our own lives, frantically trying to forge a path forward. If it helps, ask a close friend or a coworker what they perceive as your narrative and see how different it is from the one in your head.

I also decided to do a values audit to understand what my core values were and if I was living by them. Like the career ikigai tool, a values audit can help you gain clarity about the direction you're taking in work or in life. While a values audit can be as simple or complicated as you want it to be, a good way to do this is to think back to before your career even began. What did you live by when you were in school or college? What were your ideals and the means to live those ideals in your life ahead, when it wasn't shrouded by practical, financial incentives and paths? I, for example, wanted to be a writer and an economist, and to be constantly stimulated through a diversity of experience. Those are all clues for what my values were, before my ordained path started to define practical choices.

I wanted to understand if my narrative of not living by my values was in fact true. I realized my core values in life have always been authenticity, variety, and stability. This fresh understanding and externalization of my experience helped me take a more balanced view of my career so far and how I'd lived my values.

Where I got to was that, given my background, I had achieved an immense variety of experiences that I cherished in a relatively short period of time. I had also achieved longer-term financial stability very early in my career, something that seemed so unattainable given the early context of my life. By acknowledging a childhood fear, the fear of a financially insecure existence, I took away its power and worked to eliminate it. Even though I was striving for quality of work, subconsciously financial stability mattered to me immensely. I gave myself permission to feel that that was okay.

Through the diversity of roles, regions, and experiences I exposed myself to, and by bringing my most authentic self to work across those experiences, I had in fact met all three of my core values. Shifting that narrative helped me find empowering pivots for my past, present, and future—through a powerful, unbiased acceptance and acknowledgment. It helped me pivot the drivers of my experience and, thus, made the experience and mental narrative itself feel less punishing.

It also helped me think about what my choices enabled. It enabled me to be stable financially, which enabled me to take a break from a corporate career aimed at continually making more money and engage with a variety of passions. I started a photography store, wrote this book, and just did what truly made me happy. It enabled me to travel to over 60 countries by the time I was 30 and meet my American wife. It enabled me to understand the world through a diverse, macro lens. That shift from feeling drained to feeling stimulated, empowered, and grateful helped me yank myself out of the exhaustion that I felt in my daily life and be more at peace with my choices. The stability of a decade-long job at Google enabled variety far beyond my corporate career, through photography, travel, writing, and life-coaching experiences.

What the re-forming of my past narrative also gave me was a base to think about the larger meaning of future work in my own life. It helped me change how I thought about work, its place in my life, and, most importantly, how I measured success in terms of work, by readjusting my expectations and relationship with work.

Moreover, it gave me an understanding of how value systems can be evaluated and satisfied within conventional career paths. And that they should be evaluated in a constant manner to understand what you want of yourself and life, given where you are right now. I think everyone should break down their career ikigai and do a values/narrative audit every year!

While all this may not apply to your narrative or life, by finding objectivity in your own narrative without judgment and evaluating your values, you will find a more empowering narrative of your own life choices and the life you seek to build. Most importantly, changing your narrative will enable you to create synergies between your goals at work and in life, something obvious many of us in the corporate world don't think about a lot.

This is how I think about work now:

- *My work is a part of my life, an important one, yet just a part of it, just like the many other parts, and it isn't all-consuming.*

- *My work enables me to have the financial security to live my life and pursue my passions. I am not in a race up any ladder. The only race I am running is my own.*

- *I do not link my identity to a career trajectory anymore. It is linked to my values—diverse, stimulating, fulfilling work.*

- *I cherish the many experiences, the exposure, and the people that my work brings into my life.*

- *I strive to do interesting work, but I am not obsessed with having a job or profession that is perfect for me. I've accepted that it doesn't exist!*

By shifting your narrative about the larger role work plays in your life, through an anchor of your own values, you can feel better about yourself and your work in the short term.

In the long term, it will help anchor your choices about future work and career paths. For example, I am not motivated by unending salary and vertical growth anymore. I am happy with work that pays me enough to live a life of fulfillment outside of work. In corporate structures, this attitude is labeled unambitious, as the system is built on solely incentivizing vertical growth. However, by thinking about this attitude as sustainable and kind to yourself, you can allow yourself to feel that your ambition is not defined by corporate metrics, but by your own values.

PART TWO

EXPECTATION VS. REALITY FOR MILLENNIALS

MODERNITY WIDENS THE

BURNOUT HIGHWAY

CORPORATE STRUCTURES AND MASS JOB CREATION

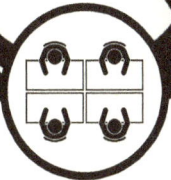

ONE-SIZE-FITS-ALL APPROACH TO WORK

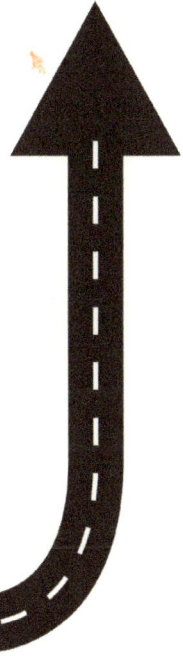

CHAPTER 4

Expectation vs. Reality for Millennials

I like to call millennials—people born between 1981 and 1996—the "bridge" or "sandwich" generation, often caught between two worlds, the old and new, the last generation that has conscious memories of the world before the internet, a generation that saw the direct fruits of a globalized world, while experiencing the pain it brought during events like the 2008 financial crisis. Due to this constant identity crisis, millennials are also often a confused, noncommittal generation.

This reflects in burnout rates too. The *2023 Workplace Burnout Survey* by Deloitte showed that 84 percent of millennials felt burned out at their jobs, as compared to 77 percent of professionals overall. In the same survey, nearly half of millennials say they have left a job due to burnout, as compared to 42 percent overall. As more baby boomers exit the workforce, in 2025, about 75 percent of the global workforce are expected to be millennials, meaning a large proportion of the workforce is prone to burnout.[1]

Much has changed as millennials grew up, seeing the dawn of a post–Cold War world, focused on unification and economic growth, fueled by liberal economic principles and a connected, more global world. As kids, millennials saw the first wave of globalism, the breaking down of boundaries after the fall of the Berlin wall, the birth of the internet, and the dot-com boom. They bought into a system that brought their parents a categorically better life than their grandparents, who were dealing with the aftermath of the Second World War and many newly independent, post-colonization, unstable states.

In the West, millennials grew up in arguably the most prosperous time in the postwar world through the '80s and '90s, with the US economy growing at about 4 percent annually through the period. In the socialist Soviet Union, the first millennials saw the fruits of capitalism around them, and started to experience it themselves with its breakup and the formation of the EU. In developing parts of Asia, countries like India liberalized economies and saw a boom through the '90s. Millennials then saw the unprecedented rise of China through the 2000s, becoming the factory of the world, built on global free trade, through capitalistic principles, driving home an economic miracle enabled by cheap manufacturing, international product dumping, and price discrimination.

So, across the world, millennials generally grew up in an optimistic economic environment, and there was reason to truly believe in the ordained path they were shown. While the cost of living and inequality rose everywhere, so did wages and

GDP growth, enabling the promise of the "American dream" to be exported across the world through the '90s.

Most of this growth, though, was funded by large, reckless government deficit spending or borrowing throughout the world. As millennials were taking up their first jobs, the 2008 global financial crisis hit, creating a black swan event, with economies around the world taking over five years to recover. While the world recovered, it was clear that there were problems. Less than a decade later, the leading proponent of free market economies and global integration elected Donald Trump twice, a hard-right, inward-looking leader, and ushered in a new era of similar global leaders over the next decade—Narendra Modi, Jair Bolsonaro, Duterte, Boris Johnson, Marine Le Pen, and so on. Millennials, within the first decade of their careers, saw the world shifting politically, taking a hard right.

This hard right was politically enabled by deficit-fueled, extremely unequal growth that was concentrated in certain sections of society, leaving a large chunk of people behind. These people, left behind by globalism, formed the vote base of right-leaning movements like MAGA (Make America Great Again) and Brexit. Also, this growth was highly concentrated in the developed countries of the West. According to the *World Inequality Report 2022*, about 50 percent of the world's poorest people share only 8 percent of the world's income, while the top 10 percent enjoy over 50 percent of it![2]

Additionally, through this period, and through the time of millennials' teenage years, growth was concentrated in certain sectors like technology, which ballooned to grow like the financial sector did in the '80s and '90s, enabling a wave of new jobs. Millennials, Gen Xers, and Gen Zers, too, were conditioned to desire high-income corporate jobs, as those became more readily available. Today, we are living in a rapidly evolving economic landscape where AI is eliminating jobs, global trade is being rebalanced, and even developed countries are starting to accept a higher degree of inflation as something inescapable, given the deficit spending of the past. Recessions triggered by events like COVID or the 2008 financial crisis demand an increase in money supply to stimulate the economy, triggering an inevitable bout of inflation.

Inflation essentially eats into the future value of money, both for income earners and asset owners. However, asset prices generally adjust more rapidly to higher inflation, as compared to worker wages. Thus, inflation widens the rift in wealth inequalities.

A combination of high inflation and low interest rates made house prices appreciate rapidly during COVID until 2023, as inflation skyrocketed in the US to 7 percent in 2021,[3] peaking at 9.1 percent in June 2022. A certain degree of inflation is important for growth, and central banks around the world carefully determine inflation targets that are healthy for their economies. In the US, the Fed's target is 2 percent. The high inflation is also one of the reasons the S&P 500 index grew about 95 percent between August 2020 and July 2025.[4] What did your average raise look like? The value of a worker's wage is likely to continue to lose more future value proportionally, as compared to assets like stocks or real estate.

With the advent of AI, that promise of even the highly profitable technology sector sustaining jobs for the duration of millennial lives has evaporated. Our concentrated economic model is crying out for diversification and development of new industries. But the extreme inequality and stubborn global political environment are making that shift in policy hard to achieve. Rather than diversifying, today's political climate is incentivizing a reversal back to the more traditional industries of the '80s and '90s.

Late-Stage Capitalism

As millennials, most of us are facing a generational challenge. Alongside conditions of late-stage capitalism, we are also faced with the existential question of what kind of world we leave our children and grandchildren.

Fredric Jameson, American literary critic and philosopher often credited with linking literature to capitalism, published a journal on postmodernism in 1991, within which he expanded the concept of late-stage capitalism to the cultural realm. In his account, this is characterized by "societies that have lost their connection with history and are defined by a fascination of the present."[5] I would argue that as a society, in addition to our past, we have lost our connection with the future too!

He also goes on to say that this stage of capitalism is characterized by "a global, postindustrial economy where everything—not just material resources and products, but also immaterial dimensions, such as the arts and lifestyle activities—become commodified and consumable. In this stage, we see innovation for the sake of innovation, a superficial projected image of self via celebrities or influencers."[6]

We are at a stage in the world where, through a global community enabled by the internet, a larger number of people are innovating for the sake of innovation. Do we really need AI to switch on our lights or make our morning coffee? In some areas, we are solving way more than we need to while completely ignoring the urgency that some other problems demand—big-tech companies are still innovating ad delivery and making short-form video delivery even more addictive while the climate crisis is ignored. Likewise, we are hyperaware of popular trends from across the world and the global capitalist webs that operate our lives and how that is destroying the world we leave our children.

What was sold to millennials as an economic system that would bring the entire world sustainable peace, prosperity, and integration is being questioned so fundamentally in the face of that larger, looming existential threat. As people working within these companies, a lot of us naturally feel that we aren't doing the best we can and are a part of the problem. That feels like a burdensome weight for a lot of us to carry, trying to balance the realities of survival with the realities of the environmental challenges that will inevitably hit future generations.

According to CompaniesMarketCap.com, the market cap of the top five companies in the world is about $14 trillion as of June 2025. All these companies are American tech companies. In fact, eight of the top ten companies by market cap are American. There are just two countries that have a larger annual GDP than the market cap of the world's five most valuable companies.[7] Corporations becoming larger than countries and having a disproportionate say in the political affairs of multiple countries across the world enforces the late-stage capitalism we live in.

As millennials, we are seeing ice caps melting and the climate rapidly changing every year—the average surface temperature on Earth has risen steadily since my birth, 1991. Storms are intensifying, seasons are becoming more and more extreme, but we're having to go back to the jobs that are making the planet terminally ill, driven by unending bottom-line dollar value growth, without any provision in accounting for societal costs.

According to the *Oil and Gas Global Market Report 2024,* the oil and gas industry raked in $8 trillion in revenue in 2023 with a projected growth of 5.7 percent over the next decade.[8]

This is happening when it is common knowledge that fossil fuel consumption is the primary reason for a warming planet. Additionally, things we were taught to trust, like recycling waste, labels like "sustainable" on foods, and so on have been proven to be a mockery. The examples are endless, from the excessive lead found in Nestle's Maggi noodles in India[9] to the deception of "sustainably" caught fish highlighted in the Netflix documentary *Seaspiracy*[10] to the largest banks and insurance companies in the world colluding with credit agencies to flood the market with high-risk securities pre-2008 (by the way, credit default swaps are still traded!).

The world is flooded with such examples of unending greed driven by systemic incentives leading to a mockery of the principles that the very system preaches. This repeated pattern isn't because corporations, or the people running those corporations, are evil. It is because greed is incentivized by the system that is the foundation of our economic setup.

According to a 2023 McKinsey & Company study, with the advent of AI, it is estimated that about 30 percent of the jobs today will be eliminated by 2030.[11] Companies are becoming leaner and AI is even threatening jobs like software development, the backbone of the immigration wave from places like India to the West.

As the technology sector consolidates its domination over every other sector in the economy through AI, there is a sense of unease, especially in young millennials and Gen Zers, of the pivot we're taking, given that larger context we live within. More and more, the current job market, rife from the unprecedented tech layoffs globally and the AI wave, has shown us that companies are, probably for the first time in history, valuing people who are good with tools and the application of tools, over people who are good with people. This is making a lot of people skills rapidly redundant in today's corporate job market.

Additionally, we haven't shifted enough jobs to sectors like environmental technology, urban planning, climate research, renewable energy, and so on to help pivot the economy and the workforce toward larger existential threats that need urgent solving. You can look at the stock market rally through 2023–2025 to see how clean energy stocks have lagged the S&P 500, and particularly AI stocks.

Even when capitalism, in its current form, reaches positive outcomes, like the electric vehicles boom in the past few years, it seems to have a sinister undertone. There is general consumer awareness and desire to act to make more sustainable environmental choices through purchasing decisions. Electric vehicles (EVs), sustainable packaging, environmentally friendly products, and so on are all part of fulfilling that buying impulse, laced with good intentions.

However, while EVs have been marketed to us as environmentally friendly, without proportional investments in cleaning up the electrical grid, they are simply currently adding additional load to a dirty grid. As of 2021, according to the US Environmental Protection Agency, natural gas and coal accounted for approximately 60 percent of US energy production, with all renewable energy accounting for about 17 percent of energy production.[12] In developing economies like India, where EVs are becoming more and more popular, about 75 percent of the country's grid is still powered by coal. Even in China, 70 percent of the grid is fueled by fossil fuels.[13]

The information asymmetry between corporations and consumers that exists in the "free market" today leads to such adverse outcomes, despite consumers, and even workers within corporations, generally wanting to do the right thing. Most consumers are oblivious to the devastating effect AI will have on the environment due to its huge power needs. And it isn't the consumer's fault—that oblivion is delivered by the unending marketing that companies do to project a force of goodness in the world.

Inequality in Late-Stage Capitalism

We know that the world has become more and more economically unequal. Additionally, increasing inflation will only increase inequalities between asset owners and income earners. But what does economic inequality make people feel? It creates a vastly different experience of the world as a poor, middle-class, or rich person, with your status and standing in society driven by the dollar amount you have. People link their identities and self-worth to increasingly unattainable dollar amounts, while social media throws exaggerated lifestyles in their faces, making them feel like failures. This creates a dangerous emotional foundation for the individual.

In a system that simply incentivizes one outcome, driven by the need for more, no matter what, the agents in the system respond to those incentives and deliver toward that. And that incentive in our system today is more money. This money-based system built on "adapt or die" mimics the natural world. However, with the sole value driver being bottom-line dollar value growth, it is killing the natural world, and, in turn, killing us.

This has also been enabled by the accounting practices we follow, which force companies to manage to a dollar value bottom line, without accounting for any environmental or social costs in any way whatsoever. Solutions like carbon credits and recycling have been sold to us as saviors but are primarily methods of greenwashing.

The carbon credits or offsets system, for example, was devised by corporations and governments in the West to be able to cheaply offset greenhouse emissions to sponsor greenhouse gas reduction projects in developing countries. This is much like how recycling was promoted by the plastic industry in the US in the 1960s, leaving the world in a fix 60 years later as Asian economies began banning single-use and microplastic imports. As Fredric Jameson said, we're living in a system defined by "a fascination of the present," kicking the can down the road in exchange for some dollar bills today.

The Gini coefficient, the most accepted metric of economic inequality globally, is constantly rising for most developed and developing economies. In 2025, South Africa, one of the high-growth BRICS countries, is the most unequal country in the world. Brazil is at number six.[14] Thus, even in economies that are growing rapidly, this concentration of wealth in the hands of a few is creating room for strife within younger populations.

As millennials and younger people, we are starting to have a general lack of trust in corporations, governments, institutions, and systems to deliver the most important current and future needs in the world.

However, our life paths have driven us toward these pillars of the capitalist political economy and we don't know how to make large-scale, systemic, collective, or individual change. And, in my opinion, there are ulterior motives for us as a generation as well. We aren't anywhere near financial security as a generation, and in the West, the wealth that was accumulated through traditional paths by previous generations is now but a pipe dream for a large proportion of the population.

According to *The New York Times,* in 2024, millennials made up about 21 percent of America's population but have just $14 trillion (about 10 percent) of the $140 trillion of accumulated wealth. In contrast, boomers (1946–64) and Gen Xers (1965–80) make up a combined 40 percent of the US population but account for a whopping $125 trillion (about 90 percent) of the wealth, with boomers accounting for half of the nation's wealth. Even the silent generation (before 1946) holds about $18 trillion.[15]

As the cost of living crisis escalated in the West through 2022–23, we saw inflation as high as 9 percent in certain sectors of the US economy. Inflation is taking the dream of home ownership further away from millions of Americans and Europeans. So, despite us as a generation constantly battling those existential questions, we don't have the basic financial security we thought would be a given growing up. This forms a danger-ous existential potion that millions of young people face every single day.

Emotional vs. Business Needs

Because of a confluence of late-stage capitalism, climate change, shifting political ideologies, and a general lack of trust in gov-ernment and industry, there is a dark cloud hanging over us, driving a feeling of "what's the point?"

There is an emotional drain we collectively feel, exacerbated by the intrusive tech and social media we surround ourselves with. The propaganda of recycling, "sustainable" labels, and individual responsibility beamed at us constantly has made us believe that small individual actions can make lasting change, a convenient position sold to us by corporations who are not incentivized to create systemic change and accountability, unless it drives more profit for shareholders. The companies and countries that sit atop this food chain continue to fool us with bottom-line fulfilling prophecies and toxic positive marketing.

And despite the emotional drain, we've accepted that we are living helplessly in a system that is designed to be unequal, concentrating wealth and resources in the hands of a few, with governments too incentivized to continuously generate dollar-value profits.

It is a system designed to serve business needs over emo-tional ones. It is a system that monetizes our restlessness and wants us to be sleepless, continuously scrolling through inun-dated feeds, being lured into buying stuff we don't need—junk food, junk goods, junk everything! It is 24/7 consumerism.

Thus, more and more, young people are trying to figure out an escape out of this system, which seems to be leading us, as individuals and a collective, to an unending treadmill of wants. Cue the rise of the creator economy, day-trader economy, the independent consultant economy, and so many other avenues that are fueling this escape.

While these avenues create opportunities for individual entrepreneurship, the working population in general, and millennials in particular, are not adapted to this shift and such lack of structure in their careers. Most millennials, and Gen Z to an extent, have been trained to look toward the conventional system that they expected to meet their needs. With uncharted mountains to climb, there is a general sense of dread about the future that grips them, and it shows in the rising rates of anxiety over the globe.

The expectations and positivity millennials grew up with has evaporated toward a realization of an existential dread we are now faced with, both at a personal and collective level. That means more and more of us are struggling to find a deeper connection with our work—the *why* behind it. That thought itself has caught many millennials unaware, without a plan for what other paths could lie ahead, leading to high levels of burnout, stress, and anxiety.

To ground this thought and experience that I know is anecdotally true for so many of us, I used the 50-plus-person survey described in the introduction to understand people's general experience at work. When asked how fulfilled they felt throughout their careers, ranging from a scale of 1 to 5 (1 being extremely fulfilled and 5 being they felt like shit about their work), about 47 percent of people said they were between

3 and 5.[16] Additionally, 33 percent of the group surveyed said "maybe" and "yes" to their job being a "bullshit job."[17] You can delve deeper into the journey of people I surveyed through the *Wide World View* podcast.

In a rancid environment like this, empowering yourself with the awareness of how you got here will lead to answers about where you want to go. And continuing to be a participant in the corporate world is a totally fair answer. Because if it comes from a place of awareness and acceptance, with an internal alignment of "the why," you are less likely to feel that debilitating tension between your expectation and reality that leads to burnout. Humans are eventually driven by "the larger why," something we tend to start ignoring as our needs are met and our careers continue to progress in a linear, upward fashion.

So, aligning your larger why continuously, even if it serves a cold rational need and suppresses an emotional one, will get you to a calmer place as you continue to climb up the corporate ladder.

CHAPTER 5

Corporate Structures and Mass Job Creation

My first job with Google was to review search ads for policy compliance and was incentivized based on the number of ads reviewed per day (productivity) without errors (quality). For that, I was paid a princely sum of about $300 a month after tax, which I can say was extremely "competitive" for the fresh-out-of-college labor market in India at the time. I essentially was a factory worker working at a desk, just in an office with free food and games.

However, I was a passionate economics graduate from one of the best arts colleges in India, who craved fulfilling work, which, at the time, I believed was just a bit further up the corporate ladder. Thus, I started my journey up the ladder, at the beginning, by reviewing at least 10,000 ads a day without errors to prove I was capable of doing better work. In a few months, I was asked to manage the team's workflow and within a year, I had moved into research-based sales support, after a promotion. At the time, it felt like I was on track for a fulfilling career focused on satisfying, meaningful work!

Every step up that ladder, for 11 years, promised fulfilling work and "better" prospects, if I just had some patience, if I met certain conditions. After sales support, the natural path was to move into insights-driven client management, which I did across a global sales organization, moving to Dublin and then Singapore in the space of three years.

While I learned a lot in terms of stakeholder management and paper pushing across large organizations, I remained unfulfilled in terms of the quality of work I was doing. My expectations of the work I thought I would be doing at this point did not match my reality. I was a slave to my inbox, my day governed by what CMOs and my clients needed from me that day. In the meantime, I was earning a wage that I had never dreamed of, even a few years before. That, and the ability to access the world, kept me grateful for my experiences. However, I also increasingly felt locked in.

That feeling of wanderlust accompanied by a pining to do fulfilling work then led me to Google New York to take up a core behavioral research role. What better way to analyze the world than Google data, I thought. While that was true, the research I was doing was to help Google eventually sell more of its own media, and unless it was helping drive a certain message, it wasn't deemed "business critical"—something that sealed the fate of our global team when we were all laid off among the "Google 12k" in 2023.

I was heading a team, rising from the bottom within eight years at the "world's best employer," and solving "critical business challenges." It just didn't feel that way to me. I was well and truly in the middle-management trap, a stage in corporate careers that is rife with burnout. I was also riddled with guilt, as I blamed myself for not being satisfied with a life that most I knew envied deeply. It felt like a generally emotionally unsustainable life.

What I have just described is a classic dichotomy in the average corporate experience today, which can be broken down into three distinct stages: early learning, middle management, and executive leadership.

How Careers Begin

The early-learning stage is where most workers are just happy to be there, fresh from the education system and internships, with job market making you feel that this is your best option. Additionally, you are learning new things, having new experiences, and, most importantly, earning a wage for the first time and enjoying the many perks that sort of independence brings. Most jobs at this stage also consist of mastering a process or a skill set that is necessary for the company. In my case that was reviewing ads and then using the many optimization templates I built to support the sales organization. Most people are in this phase for the first three to five years of their careers, hopefully getting promoted along the way.

Today, this stage usually starts with internships, an absolute must to get corporate jobs, even with graduate and postgraduate degrees. Internships provide a window into the early-learning stages of the general corporate experience around the world with a focus on learning tricks of the trade and upskilling. The trend to intern has only risen as a way of signaling your worth to the job market. According to WayUp, a job-hunting platform for college students and recent grads, more than 62 percent of the class of 2017 was doing some sort of an internship, up from 50 percent in 2008 and 17 percent in 1992.[1]

So, how did internships, which today are more like entry-level jobs, become the norm?

The adoption of modern internships as standard practice came in the 1970s, with the increase of college graduates. Moreover, those new college graduates was entering a tougher job market and the provision of internships was seen as beneficial to both parties. According to *Time,* the number of universities in the US offering programs that let students split their time between internships and regular coursework increased five-fold from 200 in 1970 to 1,000 in 1983.[2]

John Nunley, a labor economist, states that in the 1970s, one in ten people had a college degree.[3] According to Pew Research, in 2021, 38 percent of Americans over the age of 25 had a bachelor's degree, or close to four in ten, up 7.5 percent since 2011.[4] Essentially, the job market has radically changed from needing hands for production to needing minds that are critical thinkers and problem solvers. Internships are a way today to help employers gauge these skills toward future employment. A survey by Nunley and Seals found that 60 percent of internships were unpaid in 2015.[5]

And until 2018, a job that met the following six requirements in the US could legally qualify as an "unpaid internship":

- *The internship must be similar to training that would be given in an educational environment.*
- *The internship must be for the benefit of the intern.*
- *The intern does not displace regular employees.*
- *The employer derives no immediate advantage from the intern.*
- *The intern is not entitled to a job at the end of the internship.*
- *The intern understands that he or she is not entitled to wages.*

You could argue the modern internship experience increasingly does not meet this six-point criteria, especially in relation to the employer receiving direct benefits and, less so, the intern not being entitled to a job. And interns have argued the same, in court, with the famous case of two interns at Fox Searchlight Pictures who worked on the 2011 blockbuster *The Black Swan*. While they won the case in 2013, the decision was overruled in 2015, when the Court of Appeals in New York stated that the key factor is who is the "key benefactor." If it is the intern, then an internship can be unpaid.[6]

That Lonely Place in the Middle

Many large corporations resemble a bowling pin, fat around the middle, with layers of middle management vying for larger teams and layers under them. According to the US Census Bureau's statistics of US businesses, there were 19,688 businesses in the US in 2021 with over 500 employees, a loose benchmark for a large corporation. These large corporations employed approximately 69 million people of the estimated 128 million total employed, more than 50 percent of employment.[7]

According to Harvard Business School, managers made up 13 percent of the US workforce, around 17 million in 2022.[8] The layoffs in 2023–24 targeted this middle layer the most, with Google cutting nearly 10 percent of its managers and VPs, for example.[9] However, the bowling pin still remains, even if it has lost a few pounds.

After you've mastered a process or skill set during the early-learning phase, especially as a generalist, the corporate experience pushes you toward managing others through their journey of mastering the same process or skill set. This is dangled as a carrot for you, with increased responsibility, money, and perceived power. You suddenly feel like a peer of your immediate bosses and in the beginning, a sense of pride ensues.

However, this is the time when most people also start to get into the weeds of a quintessential part of corporate life—politics! Slowly, you have more access to senior leaders, often driving conflicting visions that you are trying to justify, playing their own game of thrones.

You start to have days packed with meetings, with both your team and people higher up. At this stage, you are increasingly taken away from the process or skill that you've mastered, which got you there in the first place. Your day-to-day tasks are centered on guiding employees through the process while ensuring employee satisfaction, based on driving a larger vision that is usually set by executive leadership with minimal input from you. And, that often leads to lower job satisfaction. You are literally the meat in a corporate sandwich.

This also means that middle managers are directly responsible for managing attrition in a corporation. Limeade, a corporate wellness technology company, found that managerial support was more crucial than C-level support for employee well-being.[10] However, it is also true that middle managers are the most likely to face the sack in tough times, which calls for a "flattening" of large organizations, something we have seen far too often in 2023–24. Emotionally, this threatens not just middle managers, but even people whom middle managers are most connected with, those in the early-learning stage.

Thus, as a middle manager, you're often focused on trying to learn the ropes of managing employees day-to-day while also managing up. In addition, you are learning to give up control over a skill or process that you know you can achieve better than the employees you manage. You are also expected to achieve a fine balance between employee well-being and business execution. Finally, you are also most at risk when the layoff season inevitably comes. You are often thrown into this, without much ongoing support or training.

Thus, this stage can feel lonely, frustrating, and, most of all, extremely stressful. According to a 2023 survey by the Workforce Institute at UKG across 3,400 middle managers in ten countries, some 46 percent of middle managers say they are likely to quit their jobs in the next 12 months due to "work-related stress."[11] Other surveys put this number even higher, with Microsoft's global Work Trend Index stating that 53 percent of managers in 2022 were burned out.[12]

Christina Maslach, a social psychologist and professor at UC Berkeley and a pioneer in burnout research, classifies reasons for managerial burnout into six buckets: an unsustainable workload, a perceived lack of control, insufficient rewards, a lack of supportive community, lack of values, and mismatched values and/or skills.[13] Post-pandemic, with the increase in remote work, managers also report less coaching and support, which exacerbates these problems.

While I have touched upon all these themes earlier, let's delve a bit deeper into a perceived lack of control and the mismatched values and skills. We can all agree that we derive fulfillment from something if that experience matches or exceeds the expectations we set in our minds for it. With middle management, most people have an expectation that this would afford them more control over team values, strategy, and vision, along with control of execution.

However, middle managers feel that they often execute an executive leader's vision or strategy. Given the layers in large corporate organizations, it can also feel that the executive leader doesn't have much input on how that strategy is set, either, being simply given directives from C-level leadership. There is always someone higher up driving the agenda, or the change in it.

This often creates the wrong incentives for managers of middle managers, executives focused on building their own little empires within large corporate organizations, leading to middle managers focusing on showcasing visibility-driven success stories that make their executives look good. This usually leads to a misalignment of early-stage values and skills, which is what got them the middle management jobs, especially since most middle managers who get promoted to the role excelled at their early-stage jobs.

Another path into middle management or executive leadership, depending on the size of the company, usually involves expensive postgraduate degrees to signal higher worth to the labor market. According to the Stanford Institute for Economic Policy Research, 96 percent of MBA students enter managerial positions within 15 years of receiving their degree.[14] Additionally, Wharton research found in 2012 that external hires are paid 18–20 percent more while performing worse than internally promoted employees in the first two years.[15] This creates a different sort of tension within internally promoted and externally hired middle-management peers.

How Mass Job Creation Happens

While the industrial revolution brought higher wages and prosperity, as defined by income levels, it also brought with it a breaking down of tasks to their simplest aspects via specialization, thus creating opportunity for more job creation.

The factory worker in Manchester in the 1800s and the Amazon warehouse worker and the factory worker in China building iPhones today have one thing in common—their performance depends upon executing a menial, repetitive task as efficiently and perfectly as possible under stringent conditions. While mastering screwing in a tiny part of the iPhone 5,000 times a day is good for Apple, it probably isn't good for the mental and physical health of that factory worker.

Work in an "industrialized economy," for most of the workforce, wasn't ever meant to be stimulating. Also, such jobs are most at risk of being automated, making it even worse for the worker emotionally. What AI and automation can't replace, though, is the ingenious power of human thought.

By exporting this principle of breaking down tasks into

extremely specialized jobs, in large corporations, we end up with the highly specialized world of jobs we live in today. These specialized jobs create pyramid-like structures and organizations within corporations, with workers entering such specialized processes at the bottom of the pyramid and success being defined as climbing up that pyramid, through specialized middle management and executive positions.

Customer service, for example, ropes people in at the bottom, answering emails, chats, or calls. If your own metrics are good, you then move on to managing team workflows, metrics, people, and so on. Let's look at the way customer service, a key job creator for the developing economies of Asia, is set up in most large organizations.

Think about your last customer service experience over the phone with a large corporation. I went through one with my credit card company where I had a simple question related to one of their much advertised "free benefits."

At first, I was directed to a website that claimed to have all the information I would need. Unsuccessful, I then directed my query to someone on their app through the chat feature. After being given the same links by a bot, I was finally directed to an agent. The agent then directed me to another agent who was from the team that handled the particular benefit I needed more information on.

The agent, however, said that I was chatting with them outside of working hours and thus, the people who handled that specific benefit were unavailable. I was then given a phone number and an email to get in touch with them. I decided to take a break from the process for a few hours, questioning how this experience was sold to me as free, convenient, and beneficial.

Since I was traveling abroad, I chose to email rather than call in. The email was answered promptly but directed me to the same links I started with and the same phone number I had been provided with on chat! Frustrated, I called the number, only to be recited all the benefits I was enrolled into, first by a bot and then by a young Spanish man. However, the Spanish man could not answer my query since it was before 8 a.m. Eastern time in NYC and thus, I was speaking to an employee in Spain and not the US. I'd need to speak to an agent from that team, based in the US. Twenty-four hours later, I felt like I was in an endless loop, between so many agents who had very specific geo-based and topical expertise, within one credit card company.

A few hours later, after the clock had struck 8 a.m. Eastern, I called the number again and was finally able to speak to an agent from that specific team. I felt like I had finally struck gold. However, that feeling was short-lived as I was told that the "benefit" was actually an optional product in the US that I needed to buy. There were other countries where this benefit was "free," something the reps in the other countries didn't even know! So, 48 hours later, here I was, thinking about new solutions and new customer service experiences to look forward to.

I am sure this experience is something that we are all too familiar with. I have a few unforgettable ones that I can continue narrating myself, a favorite being an experience with my phone company where they couldn't verify my identity over the phone from the Philippines, even while I stood in one of their flagship stores in New York. They couldn't even cancel my phone line without being able to verify my identity, which could only be done by someone on the phone sitting in the

Philippines, someone who had the wrong information about places I had lived in, because of a faulty database in the company's verification system. It was excruciating then, but it is simply comical since. And that's how we've created so many jobs across so many places.

Back to the credit card company example—here are all the touchpoints or jobs I went through in that 48-hour customer service experience, which could simply have been a couple of clicks on a well-designed website or app:

- *The credit card website, accessed through an ad on Google and then another organic listing, with probably multiple search agencies involved in that showing up there*
- *The five different country-specific websites of my credit card company, all probably designed by web designers across the world*
- *The app of my card company, the creation and maintenance of which also created many jobs*
- *The AI-assisted chat bot that served me the same links, which also probably created jobs*
- *The chat agent who specifically dealt with generic, simple queries over chat*
- *The agent who answered my email and gave me the same phone number and links I already had*
- *The first agent I spoke to over the phone, who couldn't answer my queries*
- *The second agent, from the specific team, who finally was like "oops, sorry!"*

- *All the supervisors (who I wanted to speak to!) across all these processes and the executives who run these customer service organizations*

This little experience, had the company truly been prioritizing customer experience, should have been extremely simple and not involved at least 15 people, with extremely specialized roles across the world that dealt with a minute piece of the process. The process, though created out of potentially good intentions, usually ends up being inefficient for the customer and terribly mind-numbing for the workers involved with the wrong incentives of getting the customer through their figurative door as quickly as possible.

If you've ever worked in a starter job in a large corporation, you've probably had an experience similar to the customer service representatives previously mentioned. Many of my friends I joined Google with were put into customer service for various products or "emails" as the teams were referred to.

As I described earlier, in my first job at Google, I was tasked with reviewing at least 10,000 search ads a day across six categories of ad policies. I usually did two to three times that and was well rewarded through monetary and nonmonetary awards, more responsibility, a promotion, and a fast track into a different process that was widely considered a step up from what was literally called "the bin" by employees, short for "approval bin," into which people were trashed. It was either "emails" or the "bin" for most non-engineering entry-level employees at Google at the time.

Thus, while I was an expert at passing decisions on search ads in less than one second for dings across the six specific policies I was a master at, I had little knowledge of the 30-plus other policy categories and many other ad formats, or how those policies were even framed.

Up the chain, our middle managers were trying to implement made-up performance metrics and refine or improve our processes, often trying to justify why they must exist and be expanded for "business continuity" or "impact." They drew up performance assessments along a 25-point rating scale from 2.5 to 5 and often had to have long conversations every quarter, based on arbitrary guidelines about why you were a 3.3 versus 3.4 or 3.5. It wasn't fun, for anyone involved.

There was also a large team of reviewers sitting in another office whose only job was to check a sample of our decisions for quality. All of us were recruited as the brightest minds from campuses across India and told we were going to "do cool things that matter." We were all even given T-shirts that said that. There was a clear mismatch between that expectation and the reality. Yet, the free food, the swanky offices, and the paycheck with a promise that we'd "eventually do cool things that mattered" kept most of us there. Friends over at engineering were doing similar things, but just reviewing code.

And above our managers were executive leaders, with packed days of meetings and corporate travel, endlessly talking into their screens, indoors all day, trying to play the right cards for their little empires and set collaboration principles across the different teams, involved in a little piece of the larger process, justifying why they continuously needed more and more headcount to expand their empire, convincing someone up above that theirs was in fact a more critical empire than someone else's.

At every step in this chain, in the large corporation experience, most people are dealing with extremely specialized problems and specialized processes. You could switch teams and organizations within large corporations, but usually, it just involves switching to another specialized process. This switching also gets harder as you entrench yourself in a certain process, and it is generally the hardest for middle management, whose struggles I've explored earlier, often leading to significant burnout and exhaustion at this stage.

Add to this the fact that most of these jobs involve sitting for six to ten hours a day at a desk, indoors, with little activity and you can see why it is a recipe for burnout. Humans for thousands of years have evolved to work by applying both their mind in conjunction with their muscles. The earliest farmers had to problem-solve and understand the turning of the seasons, the suitability of the soil for various crops, the ideal crop mix and groundwater availability. They then had to build or procure tools to accomplish tasks like tilling the land, irrigating it, sowing crops, and finally harvesting them.

Similarly, potters or tool makers need to understand the availability of soil, metals, and raw materials, and then apply their strength toward various applications. An artisan weaving complicated textiles needs to understand the different fibers, inks, dyes, tools, and techniques required to get to a complex end product. A fisherman needs to understand the turning of the tides, migratory patterns of various fishes, fishing techniques available to him, and, most importantly, how to sail effectively.

Contrast how stimulating and diverse these problems are versus the little process in that large organization of yours that you're trying to master! Humans need to feel stimulated and feel a sense of connection to work, to be motivated, something we seemed to have forgotten.

Despite most of us feeling that the way we work is how we have always worked, compared to civilized human history, the age of the industrial revolution only accounts for about 3 percent of the 10,000 years or so since humans became settlers. We've been farmers, potters, and artisans for much longer than we have worked in offices. We are simply not evolved enough yet to enjoy continuously repetitive tasks that don't engage our mental and physical aptitudes.

While farmers, potters, artisans, and metallurgists still exist, any economics student would tell you that, today, economic development involves a country going through a cycle of shifting rural labor to urban, industrial sectors. Nonindustrial jobs have been de-marketed and associated with a lower status in society. Additionally, most of those jobs have also been mechanized, reducing the need for muscles, and involve more desk/sitting work. The point is, most "jobs" up until the industrial revolution challenged both the mental and physical aptitudes of humans, and many jobs today don't do that, especially physically.

Humans were designed to expect mental and physical stimulation during tasks for fulfillment. However, today, most work and roles aren't designed for that, but workers often go in with misaligned expectations, especially at the early stages of their careers.

This cycle of misaligned expectations, the lack of physical work and connection with the actual work your team is doing only gets exacerbated as you enter the executive leadership phase. This phase begins with a satisfying feeling of "I've made it" but brings with it many of the challenges of middle management, with a much sharper focus on visibility and organizational politics.

As a middle manager, you still have a day-to-day connection with the work being done through project supervision and employee management. As an executive leader, you are reduced to key talking points, constantly in charge of crafting and driving a politically motivated narrative. Not being up for that brings many emotional challenges.

The Evolution of an Organization

Specialism across processes is viewed as a natural evolution of an organization and an economy, with large-scale job creation. Usually, there is a lot more to solve when an economy or an organization is in its infancy. When I joined Google in 2012, for example, at about 25,000 employees globally, there were immense process and organizational challenges across all functions. There was a lot to solve in a rapidly growing company, and employees were rewarded when they innovated by creating new tools or processes, or streamlined collaboration challenges.

Over time, as the organization evolved, systems and collaboration processes got better with a growing realization that there were now too many tools and too many teams doing the same, or very similar, things. This set off a reverse cycle of consolidation, and incentives were drawn up for that reversal. So, there were jobs created to consolidate tools and systems and people were rewarded for "process-ifying," the opposite of what they were incentivized to do earlier.

Thus, the same organization that was rewarding people for bite-sized innovation now expected process compliance, consolidation, and coordination. Innovation was suddenly deemed a waste of time! This was sold as a business-driven need and evolution to the employees, which it was. However, people hired with an innovation mindset were now forced into a completely opposite mindset, with an expectation that they should be enjoying this too. It was just business.

Once there is consolidation and compliance across tools, teams, and processes, the organization usually demands a focus on execution, with employees rallying in an execution mindset. Once an organization masters this phase, it then tends to focus on automation for further efficiency and profit. For example, the job I and 600 others did eight years ago is done by a button in a system today.

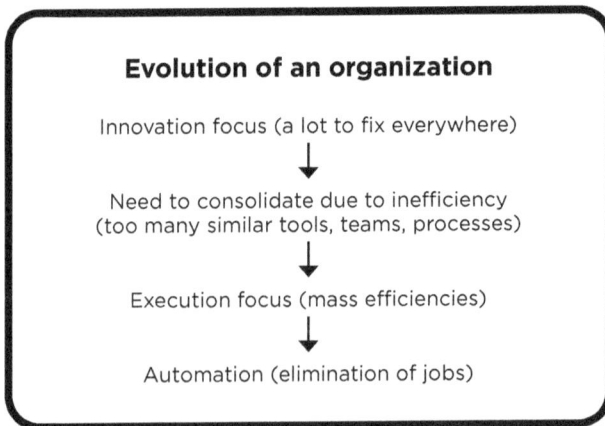

Evolution of an organization

Innovation focus (a lot to fix everywhere)

↓

Need to consolidate due to inefficiency
(too many similar tools, teams, processes)

↓

Execution focus (mass efficiencies)

↓

Automation (elimination of jobs)

To manage this evolution without much strife, most corporations have large learning and development organizations that are tasked with helping a workforce evolve with the business. Most employees within corporations are given opportunities to upskill through corporate training and executive programs. These are designed to support them through transitions in tools, processes, and an evolution of the organization that impacts their roles and day-to-day.

Job Creation and Political Power

Such specialism within generalism is the secret to modern mass job creation. Low rates of corporate tax and lower wages are used to incentivize companies to come to developing markets and create jobs, helping corporations with a larger buffer of profits, with corporations who create the most jobs often rewarded with immense political power.

As per its annual report, Google today employs 180,000-plus people globally and over 5,000 people in Dublin,[16] another office I worked in between 2015 and 2017. For context, Dublin is a city of about 500,000 people. An entire area of the city around the many Google offices is dubbed the "Google Ghetto" by locals.

To allow Googlers to cross the street without their coats in the harsh, rainy Dublin weather, the company wanted to build a pedestrian bridge across Barrow Street (often called Google Street) to connect the two main buildings. However, the bridge needed to be tested to see if anything would stand in the usual 35–50 mph gusts that knock people off their bikes and force them to hold on to pillars while walking to and from work.

To do that, Google was allowed to close down the whole street to traffic and put up a temporary structure for weeks to test the feasibility of the idea. There are other bridges like this across Google's offices in cities like New York where it employs over 10,000 people.[17] In addition, Googlers regularly had town halls where there were discussions around Ireland's immigration policies and how that could be made more friendly toward the many tech workers from all over looking to find a base in the EU.

Thus, as an organization becomes larger and larger and employs more people in local, especially developing economies, the organization gets to influence more of the local policies. In Hyderabad, another campus I worked in, Google has about 11 buildings and employs about 25,000 "vendors" or extended workforce and over 1,500 full-time employees. They are now building a 30,000-people campus on the outskirts of the city, which will bring immense development to the area and people from all over. An entire area of the city, in the last 20 years, has developed as "Cyber-abad" and employs over a million people reveling in the outsourcing boom that India has enjoyed since the early '90s.

The story has been similar in places across Southeast Asia and now parts of Africa, luring companies with even cheaper rates of labor as other economies develop and have slightly higher wages. However, many of these jobs involve being one of those customer service representatives or dealing with a very small piece of a very large puzzle, often at odd hours, for "competitive wages." Monetarily, it is better than what people would make otherwise and that means both people and governments view it as a good deal.

This sets in motion an endless cycle of burnout, especially in developing economies where there is generally a higher tolerance for burnout and mental health challenges, with lower levels of societal self-actualization. People are okay working and commuting longer hours for lesser pay and benefits because there are simply more people that would snap up what they have. A further recent rise in consumerist attitudes, especially in Asia, only makes the corporate world more attractive, even with rising burnout. The individual has no option but to find ways of coping with this emotionally.

The Age of Creativity

Every breakthrough or piece of technology has acted as a bridge to the next breakthrough in technology. We are at a point in human history where the lines between the real and virtual world are blurring. Screens have taken over our lives, and we are almost at a point of looking at our screens for sustenance. So, the question to ask is, what is this a bridge to?

The next stage in this oneness with technology will be spatial computing, integrating the space around you as an interface, which will include your hands, walls, or blank spaces around you. What this oneness has brought with it is the rise of social media and the creator economy.

With cloud computing, data, and storage becoming so cheap and internet adoption being global, everyone needs to be a creator today. We see everything from wars to pandemics to fashion trends unfold via smartphone lenses uploaded at a rate of knots, driven by the opportunity of virality. With AI, the creator economy is only booming further. Various studies put AI content already forming at least 10 percent of all new content produced on social media in 2024.

There are YouTube creators with more than a billion views and sports stars on Instagram with over 600 million followers. Only two countries have a bigger population, India and China! In India, for example, with almost 45 percent youth (20–24) unemployment in 2024,[18] nearly everyone has turned to Instagram reels or YouTube or the many other local social platforms to tap into the creator economy, both out of boredom and necessity. My 62-year-old mother, for example, sings old Bollywood covers on an app called StarMaker and has 40,000-plus followers on it. Funnily, India also has the highest number of "selfie deaths" in the world.[19]

What this lure of social media and the creator or blogger/vlogger economy does is disincentivize corporate work and vocation-based paths that have existed for so long. What more and more specialism also indicates in the world is fewer and fewer basic problems to generally solve across the world.

Think about it: A 100 years ago, we didn't have accurate maps for most places in the world, and today we have Google Maps and Street View in the palm of everybody's hands. Zoom back 300 years or so, and the British were only just getting the maps to sail to India. The basis of colonization was better cartography and shipbuilding.

Just 30 years ago, we were waiting days to get a message across the world, and today, it is instantaneous. Two hundred years ago, most of the world lived in unsanitary conditions, without sewage systems, and today, most of the developed world drinks straight out of a tap. To invest in the stock market even three decades ago, you needed a broker executing your orders via paper shares, charging fees for every transaction, and today, apps like Robinhood have truly democratized retail investing by making it app-based, free, and instantaneous.

Like organizations evolving toward more menial tasks and automation, the world has gotten to a place where there aren't as many basic things to solve. Yes, many of us are working to colonize the Moon and Mars, but an increasingly larger proportion of us are not going to do much beyond create funny reels, unless the economy pivots to solving problems we need to solve today, like climate change and urban design.

Additionally, with AI, we are getting to a new stage of evolution where most menial jobs will be automated through AI and robotics. That leaves most of us free to engage ourselves in the creator economy, even more than we do already. I truly believe that the next decades will be defined by groundbreaking creativity across the host of platforms that are yet to emerge.

No matter what you do, you need to be a creator today. Just look at your LinkedIn feed to see how desperately corporate workers are trying to be creators. I have been asked by recruiters and my publisher about why I don't engage more on LinkedIn. Having an online presence, in addition to mastering vocational skills, is not optional anymore. Already, marketing textbooks from even a decade ago need to be tossed as they don't account for social media and virality, which now drive almost everything in this digitally obsessed world.

With these trends exacerbating in the next century, companies will need fewer people to execute tasks, thus flattening corporate structures, and workers will delve into the creator and entrepreneur economy. What that will do to societal stability and welfare policies across the world is another conversation, but that is a collective challenge that governments across the world will need to solve.

With 8 billion people today, we are still on track to continue growing population numbers till about 2060, mostly driven by Africa. Africa will also be affected by climate change the most. Thus, ensuring Africans have enough to eat and stable lives, in the face of complex climate, technological, and geopolitical changes, will be the biggest test of the age of the industrial world. What this will surely trigger is a shifting of workers to other sectors, urban farming for example (hydroponics is a growing field) or urban planning or environmental technology. However, what is clear is that the world will not need as many workers as it does today.

While the creator and AI economy has the potential of lowering rates of burnout across the general population, as working for yourself brings more connection with your work, it is clear corporations are looking at it to build efficiency and stronger bottom lines. AI reduces the need for people in every established industry, especially in the largely oligopolistic big-tech sector. The World Economic Forum's *Future of Jobs Report 2025* suggests corporations are looking to cut 90-plus million jobs by 2030, while creating 170 million more.[20] Based on the evidence so far, the job creation number looks farcical. McKinsey, in 2022, estimated 70 percent of the global workforce's time spent could be replaced by AI by 2030.[21]

Thus, the AI economy is also sure to bring about different global challenges in terms of standard and quality of lives. As humans, we've pegged the emotional quality of our lives to material comforts. The current state of the labor market, inflation, and economic outlook, along with the imperative need to cut our consumption habits, promises to pose a perfect emotional cocktail, especially for the corporate worker caught in the middle of a moral dilemma.

As a corporate worker, you must keep in mind that the corporate ladder, its structures, and the basis of modern job creation itself are not designed toward personal fulfillment or empowerment. It is you who will have to find ways to engage with pockets of the corporate world that may be rewarding to you. Or find an escape within the creative economy!

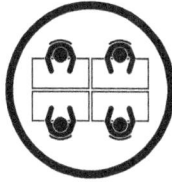

CHAPTER 6

One-Size-Fits-All
Approach to Work

The working day for corporations has become pretty standardized across the world. It usually involves a commute to an office three to five days a week, official working hours between 9 a.m. to 5 or 6 p.m., usually working at a desk on a computer, with meetings interspersed through the day, a lunch break, and a commute back. While this was challenged by remote work and COVID, the return to office push has meant we are back, fully or partially, to this standardized model, even as companies harped about productivity gains while remote.

There is little cultural nuance incorporated within the workday, and this one-size-fits-all approach can also be expanded to how benefits, salaries, and organizational structures are created within corporations across the world. Corporate culture is also usually dictated by the company's headquarters, with other regions trying to adapt and adopt a macro culture set by people sitting across the world. Thus, all in all, the corporate experience is set up very similarly whether you work in the US, Europe, Asia, or Africa.

The Missing Cultural Nuance in Corporate Work

With more globalized jobs and teams, there are often calls and meetings during "nonworking hours" that one is expected to take to be a "team player." Workers are usually incentivized through raises or promotions, and, if you're lucky, some standard global perks like health insurance, a gym membership, or a sponsored happy hour.

Global corporations have tried to adopt more local outlooks to their office spaces, or, as at big-tech companies, their lunches and happy hours. However, most of the core HR policies in global corporations are set centrally and only slightly modified to suit local markets. In markets where talent is at a premium, there is more of an incentive to accommodate for local cultural nuances. Global corporations, though, will never get to a point where they account for siestas in Spain or *wushui* (noon naps) in China. A corporation like Google has offices in 170 cities and 60 countries. Accounting for various cultural nuances to suit every single market for a global corporation is simply not feasible. This is despite noble efforts made at companies like Google to try to localize office environments to a large extent.

That means large corporations tend to have a certain feel and culture that is often driven by the country or even the region within the country it is from—the headquarters. Googlers around the world often refer to Google as being an extremely Californian company. Samsung, for example, is extremely Korean. Reliance is extremely Indian. What this usually means is an extension of the work culture and often leadership from the home nation with workers from other parts trying to integrate. This also usually means a centralization of the most important functions in their headquarters.

I spent over a decade in global roles at Google, working from offices in Ireland, Singapore, New York, and Mumbai. Given the centralization of product teams in Mountain View, California, this meant a constant struggle in trying to find equitable ways to respect each other's time while having meetings with the "most important folks" who were based in California. A big part of the work culture in California is protecting your time as your own beyond the workday, with most wanting their meetings done between 10 a.m. to 4 p.m. This meant that for those of us in places like Singapore or India, used to working outside office hours, it was very common, and accepted, to be on calls and meetings late at night or very early in the morning. I've joined meetings at 2 and 5 a.m.!

Another aspect considered extremely positive, especially in the US, is speaking in meetings. Asians generally assign a lower importance to the value of speaking versus listening. Add to it the odd times at which some of these meetings occured, and it usually led to inefficient and often unpleasant takeaways on both ends.

While there were trainings and efforts made to bridge these cultural dynamics, those bridges often ended up being nonsensical procedural fixes that tried to add structure to an unsolvable problem: time zone differences. In the end, despite the best intentions, the dominant culture of the HQ prevailed.

Additionally, most important events with leadership that were seated out of California, like "town halls" or "all hands" or the famous Google "TGIFs," were at odd hours for a lot of the Asian workforce. This left a large section of the workforce alienated, almost feeling like they were there to execute on a Californian mandate. This was also the case when a particular problem demanded a local solution or innovation, with us often having to work through incredible HQ red tape, trying to convince people on solutions they didn't understand, as they didn't have context on local challenges in distant markets.

What this means is that the company you work for will most likely not design itself around your cultural nuances. If you're used to taking naps in the afternoon and you aren't in a Spanish company, too bad! If you're from a culture that usually starts and ends work later, too bad if you find yourself in a Korean or Japanese company that values presenteeism.

Burnout and Happiness around the World

Research on burnout at a global scale is limited, and thus, it is hard to empirically study burnout rates globally, especially through the lens of our experience at corporations. However, a study by Savvy Sleeper (Sleep Junkie) that I touched on in chapter 3 standardized the largest city and country level data for seven key health- and work-related categories (ILO data), including the percentage of population sleeping less than seven hours, percentage of stressed Glassdoor reviews, time spent in traffic to/from work, mental health issue prevalence, and employee presenteeism to rank 69 cities across 53 countries in terms of burnout.[1]

Comparing Burnout Rates in Major Cities

Least Burned-Out Cities	Score (/10)	Most Burned-Out Cities	Score (/10)
Tallinn, Estonia	2.42	Tokyo, Japan	6.47
Ljubljana, Slovenia	2.70	Mumbai, India	5.95
Oslo, Norway	2.96	Seoul, South Korea	5.92
Sofia, Bulgaria	2.99	Istanbul, Turkey	5.87
Copenhagen, Denmark	3.07	Manila, Philippines	5.51
Barcelona, Spain	3.12	Jakarta, Indonesia	5.29
Amsterdam, Netherlands	3.13	Hanoi, Vietnam	5.28
Bucharest, Romania	3.13	Taipei, Taiwan	5.23
Frankfurt, Germany	3.24	Los Angeles, USA	5.17
Prague, Czech Republic	3.25	Buenos Aires, Argentina	5.12

(Source: Sleep Junkie, ILO data, Glassdoor reviews)

While the study isn't perfect, it shows us some interesting trends and causes for burnout. It is clear that European cities and specifically Western Europeans are facing the least amount of burnout in the world. On the contrary, Asians and Americans are at the highest risk of burnout. London, like its American cousins, is the only Western European city that ranks at par with American and Asian cities, with a score of 5.

Tallinn, Estonia, the least burned-out city in the world according to this study, offers an average of 29.1 days of paid vacation a year and only 5.6 percent of its population worked more than 48 hours a week in 2023.

In contrast, in the US, according to ILO data, 14 percent of the employed work more than 48 hours a week, generally two times more than most Western European countries. And Bangladesh was the highest at 50 percent of the employed working more than 48 hours a week.[2]

Percentage of Workers Working More Than 48 Hours a Week in 2023

Asia, LATAM, and Africa		Europe and the US	
Bangladesh	50%	US	14%
Pakistan	42%	Italy	9%
China	30%	Spain	7%
India	26%	France	7%
Mexico	28%	Slovenia	7%
Kenya	39%	Sweden	6%
Egypt	30%	Norway	5%

(Source: United Nations ILO Labor Force Survey data 2023)

Economic prosperity clearly seems to have a link with burnout rates and normal working hours. However, under the hood, economic prosperity brings better working culture and a more nuanced relationship with work itself. Notice how the lowest rates of burnout occur generally in Scandinavia and Western Europe, regions that were the first to develop through the industrial revolution and are not as concerned with things like employee presenteeism. Additionally, this prosperity brings with it a confidence in a particular way of life, something Western Europe clearly demonstrates.

Western Europeans actively and unapologetically substitute work and the opportunity to make more money with things that add more quality to their lives—like siestas or naps in the afternoons, early drinks by the canal, or a morning swim in the ocean rather than answering emails. They've accepted it as part of culture and identity, and thus do not view such behaviors as out of the ordinary. Similar practices by workers in the Americas or Asia induce internal guilt associated with shirking.

Today, corporate workers globally have between 8 to 25 days of annual leave across the world. According to Expedia's annual *Vacation Deprivation Report,* Americans, on average, take 11 days of vacation a year, the worst in the world.[3] And you often start a corporate job without any vacation days for the first year in the US. For comparison, a medieval peasant would have probably given himself 120 days off during a harsh winter and spring for rest and recuperation!

The exceptions to low vacation days exist usually in places across Europe. France, for example, has a minimum of 30 days of annual leave. Additionally, if you've ever worked in Europe or with Europeans, you know that August is a bad time to try to get any work done because most are on holiday for at least two weeks. Traditionally, factory plants in Germany would shut down in August, making most of the economy, which was linked to them, also go on vacation.

Another reason why Europe tends to show higher levels of happiness and lower levels of burnout is their belief in rest and recuperation, often at the expense of work or making more money—a more relaxed form of capitalism, if you will. In places like Spain, France, and Italy, it is quite common to see towns totally deserted through the afternoons, with small businesses shuttering up to take an afternoon nap. It is also quite common to find many businesses, open or not, have inaccurate hours on Google, a cardinal sin for a physical business in the US!

When I moved to Dublin, which isn't as "European" by any stretch, I was shocked to find that most shops shut around 5 or 6 p.m. I often had to make time in the middle of my workday for an errand. Being from India where everything is open as late as 11 p.m., this was quite a shock. The stores were completely unapologetic about closing so soon—in hindsight, rightly so. However, my first thought at the many experiences I had setting up my life in Dublin was that this was all a bit inefficient, something many Americans feel about Europe too. But efficiency probably isn't their first priority.

A number of Western European countries also focus on helping people actively fight the path that a vocational education usually puts you on. The state incentivizes young adults to diversify their interests well into ages that places like America and India tend to consider "old." In Sweden, for example, it is quite common to collect welfare payments till the age of almost 30 years. According to the Eurydice data network, in addition to all education, books, and food being free, this is because Sweden has grants for SEK 840 per week or $82 for every full-time student in university for a period of six years. There are also interest-free repayable loans of up to SEK 1,932 per week or $175 per week that students can bank upon for six years.[4]

It is no surprise that fulfilling concepts like "hygge," a Scandinavian concept for a "cozy space," or *gezellig*, a Dutch concept popularized by the show *Ted Lasso* for "a warm, fuzzy feeling or gathering," originate across Europe. Another fun one is the Scottish concept of "hurkle-durkle"—staying in bed lounging when you should be up accomplishing things. I've yet to discover similar concepts originating in the US.

This points to three basic tenets that Europeans adopt, which are lacking in the US and Asia, to feel more fulfilled in the paths they choose, no matter what that path is:

- *A belief in the fact that you don't need to unendingly make more money every single year—a belief instilled in Europeans who saw economic success earlier than other regions, and one driven into us through bottom-line-driven capitalism*
- *A belief that money is a means and not an end—the end is the ability to take naps every afternoon*
- *A belief in your own way of life—as an individual or a culture (Spaniards unapologetically love their siestas and bull fights)*

Logically, then, when looking at the *World Happiness Report,* which since 2002 statistically looks at happiness across the world, we see Western European nations rank highly. The report uses Gallup polling data monitoring performance across quantitative and qualitative measures—GDP per capita, social support, healthy life expectancy, freedom to make life choices, generosity of the populace, and perceived corruption levels.

In 2023, Finland was the happiest country in the world and of the top ten, eight countries were Western or Northern European, except for Israel and New Zealand. Finland has occupied the top spot for six years in a row, with Denmark usually at number two and Iceland at number three. Of the top 50 happiest countries in 2023, 30 are European, eight are Asian, and seven are North and Central American. Afghanistan is by far the least happiest in the world, ranking at 142. India, my homeland, isn't much better at 132.[5] Thus, at least as far as we can measure, Western and Northern Europeans are winning at happiness, and thus, you can argue, at life too!

What's more interesting is the inequality of happiness trends or the happiness gap, as defined by the report. It measures the difference in reported average life evaluation across the six measures between the top (happier) and bottom (sadder) halves of a country's population, essentially giving us a read on the happiness inequalities between the top and bottom halves of the country.

In Finland, the Netherlands, and Afghanistan, at opposite ends of the spectrum, the gaps are the smallest, implying the happier and sadder halves of the population have very little deviation in their perceived happiness. Even by this measure, European countries show more equality in happiness with the usual suspects being in the top 20.

However, the US falls from number 16 (down two since 2022) in the list of happiest countries to 34 when looking at the happiness gap, indicating a more unequal experience with happiness. This gap is starker in the large, developing economies of Asia with countries like Indonesia, the Philippines, Bangladesh, Pakistan, India all showing large happiness gaps.

Thus, the US and Asia have wider happiness gaps, implying income and wealth inequalities play a more prominent role than they do in Europe in defining happiness, or simply, their experience of life. This could be due to many reasons, but mostly because resources are harder to access for poorer populations, especially in developing economies.

The Money and Happiness Equation

It is well accepted that like most goods, the marginal utility derived from money or wealth diminishes with more of it. Put simply, if you are craving some chocolate, the utility or satisfaction or happiness you derive from the first piece will be the highest and will keep on declining with every next piece.

After certain lifestyle goals are achieved, your satisfaction will peak with money, like any other product you have owned. However, like chocolate, you may want way more or less money than your peers. That number may be higher or lower, based on you and the life you want, something I would think our education systems and individualistic societies should teach us to assess. However, were you ever told to evaluate what amount of money would make you happy? If you were, thank the person who gave you that perspective when you were young! Most of us, especially from working-class families, don't start thinking deeply about our finances and our relationship with money itself till well into our 30s, at best.

This lack of perspective about what money means to you and your life, along with the sole carrot of the upward ladder that corporate life dangles in front of us, is a core part of the one-size-fits-all design of the corporate experience. The whole performance and incentives system is designed around the belief that everyone in the workforce is motivated endlessly to make more money and climb the ladder. The systems are also designed to gradually push out the ones who aren't motivated by these incentives after a certain point. Horizontal movement within organizations is harder beyond a certain seniority, baking you into the upward path, with high opportunity cost off-ramps involving massive career changes.

At Google and most big-tech companies, once you're a mid-level employee, you are financially more comfortable than 99 percent of the general population by every metric, barring one. That metric is how much people around and senior to you make. When I joined Google, anecdotally, the average duration of a promotion was about 2.5 years and that slowly increased to 3.5 years.

The more junior you were, the quicker you were expected to get promoted. There were many unconfirmed stories of people being forced out since they stagnated for years at a particular level, even if performance at that level was acceptable. The graph had to go up and to the right; it could be horizontal for a bit, but not forever.

I joined the company in a batch of 45 kids straight out of college, and every two weeks over four months of summer, a new wide-eyed batch joined. That made it feel like a large class in a college every year, who were then working and competing with one another, serving as each other's benchmark. Given this was repeated every year, it fostered amazing camaraderie, having a net positive effect on work culture. It also gave every batch goals to aspire to or examples of who not to become, creating in-built benchmarks within the group. Moreover, you could also compare your performance and trajectory with people who joined a year or two before or after you.

For some people, this created an unhealthy rat race with a prioritization of vertical growth within a super-specialized space that might exist just at Google. Thus, even though people progressed vertically, they felt like they hadn't learned much experientially and were stuck. Yet, they were locked in, for the lack of a better alternative. This would then hurt them in the middle of their careers when AI and the layoffs came around. This was because they had little knowledge of the world outside the process they handled and had lost their ability to be nimble.

Based on anecdotal experience interacting with people across corporate jobs over the world, many feel stuck because, in addition to not having let themselves wander at the start of their careers, people are unclear of what role money plays in their lives and at what point will it start diminishing. This should be a key part of university curriculum, but it serves society well to leave this to the individual—so that they can continue to earn more income and pay more income taxes!

This is something all of us should spend time evaluating, based on the journey we've made, and, more importantly, the path we want to forge ahead. Realizing that wealth is an important factor in defining the happiness gap, both at an individual and collective level, is important. However, it is critical to also understand that your emotional fulfillment from wealth will eventually diminish. Having perspective on money being a means to build the life that makes you happy, rather than an end, will lead to longer-term emotional sustainability with your work and money.

The Role Taxation Plays in Wealth Distribution and Equality

It is clear that wealth and income inequality drive a more unequal experience of the world. The wider happiness gaps that exist in places like the US and developing economies are primarily driven by wealth inequalities. Taxation is the primary tool governments can use to reduce such inequalities through redistribution.

Americans, especially Gen Xers and boomers who saw better monetary returns, often balk at the "welfare-driven" or "socialist" Europeans, who usually pay higher taxes. Conversely, Eastern European friends who experienced communism also balk at it, and have migrated to places like America, Dubai, Singapore, Hong Kong, and Australia for better returns for their work and investments. And better taxation, of course.

Western Europeans, politically, have striven for a more equal society, where wealth gaps don't widen happiness gaps, even though this noble notion of equality at home was enabled by the redistribution of colonial plunder. Thus, like happiness, wealth inequality (Gini coefficients) across Western Europe is much lower than in the US, Latin America, or Asia.

A difference in attitude throughout the US and Europe shows up in how both cultures look at their billionaires. In the US, stories like that of Bill Gates, Jeff Bezos, Warren Buffett, Mark Zuckerberg, and so on are called out as stories of intense hard work leading to a proportionally intense reward. While no one makes billions without hard work and brilliance, the more troubling aspects of billionaires are generally more ignored in American society.

According to *Forbes,* 41 of the top 100 wealthiest people in the world in 2024 are Americans.[6] Climbing that ladder and climbing it quickly gives you a societal status. In Europe, that is a more nuanced concept, and Europeans generally believe that such obscene wealth should be shared more widely and not individually accumulated. That is because Europeans have also had such obscene wealth the longest. Thus, as a society, they have been at this redistribution idea longer. America was created for unchecked capitalism, and any redistribution is deemed to be too close to socialism.

This difference in attitude shows up in how taxation works in Europe versus the US. Firstly, income tax is much higher across Western Europe, up to 56 percent for the top bracket earners in Denmark, for example. According to TaxFoundation.org, Western European nations range between 45 percent to 55 percent for the top earners while the top 1 percent in America, according to federal tax data in 2020, paid approximately 25 percent on average. Switzerland had the lowest tax rate in Western Europe at 23 percent.[7]

We all saw how important taxation as an issue was during the 2024 presidential election. Naturally, nobody wants to pay a higher tax bill. However, some societies are better at accepting a more equitable tax base and a higher individual tax bill—for what it ensures for the collective.

This principle ends up being even more extreme with equity compensation, a mechanism used by billionaires to stash away their money tax-free. It is the mechanism that enables CEOs to claim to not take a salary as it is tax efficient to draw their compensation through equity, and the benefit of lower capital gains taxation. Capital gains taxes in Europe ranged from 42 percent in Denmark to about 15 percent in Greece. I paid 52 percent on stock vesting in Ireland.[8]

In the US, capital gains taxes range only from 0 percent to 20 percent federally, and you could be paying zero under a certain taxable income limit. Every dollar in capital gains is taxed at a lower rate than income and thus becomes tax efficient after a certain level of wealth.

This general tolerance for higher taxes, despite per capita incomes being lower in Europe, comes from a general belief that Western Europeans want better public infrastructure and welfare along with more universal access to resources for the entire collective. In Denmark, you pay some of the highest tax rates in the world, but education and health care are totally free, like in all of Scandinavia. All of this adds up toward creating a more equitable experience across the population, and a thus higher level of individual and collective fulfillment.

In the US, even if you go bankrupt, it is next to impossible to write off student loans (which is why Biden tried to forgive up to $20,000 of student debt for certain income levels). And, even after paying exorbitant amounts for health insurance, you often end up paying double what you'd pay in Western Europe. It is also not uncommon to pay three or four bills over months for the same medical service in the US, something I have never been able to understand, but is accepted as a standard experience by so many Americans. Because this is the only system they know!

This attitude toward taxes in Western Europe has ensured more collectivism and a higher level of welfare for all. And maintaining this delicate balance is key for Europeans, something that shows up in the vehement opposition to more refugees in especially the Mediterranean countries of Europe.

Generally speaking, though, humans will, collectively and individually, gravitate toward a system that works for them, one where the incentives align. It is because of the accumulation of wealth through colonization, funded by early stock exchanges, that Europe is now more welfare-driven. It isn't out of nobility that only Europeans were bestowed with. And it is because of the collapsing "American dream" that you see more opposition in America from younger generations against the system, as I discuss in chapter 4.

Given the history of colonization by many Western European countries of large parts of South America, Africa, and Asia, that means, in modern times, there has been a lot of wealth to go around and redistribute. The colonists needed the buy-in of the general public at home to ensure that they could continue to sponsor more infrastructure projects like canals, bridges, ports, and railways in the extractive colonies. This was done through wealth distribution and a welfare-driven mindset that continues to this day. Thus, colonization also demanded collectivism and cooperation in the mother country. You could argue that, since the Second World War, this mindset has hurt the Europeans as colonial wealth has started to dry up, and mother economies without extractive colonies haven't grown as rapidly.

In the US, it was the opposite, as a new country of immigrants, mostly from Europe and for whom the European welfare system didn't work, wanted a land that rewarded them directly and proportionally for their work and output. That is fundamental in understanding why European and American attitudes to work are so contrarian and how we got to the oft-quoted idea that Americans "live to work" while Europeans "work to live."

Asia and Its Ever-Evolving Struggle with Capitalism

As we discussed earlier, most global corporations fail to accommodate cultural nuance in planning for their workforce, unless they need to. In the past, in extractive colonies of Asia, for example, labor laws were generally weaker than the luxuries afforded to those in Europe. Additionally, the numbers game and the economic realities of developing nations meant concepts like *karoshi* or "death by work" originated in places like Japan. Given Eastern cultures have always been more inclined toward a focus on spirituality and the collective as compared to the West, it often puts their economic realities and ambitions at odds with what they want to be doing.

Fundamentally, Western philosophy generally focuses on individuality and making oneself capable, in order to then conquer worldly challenges. On the other hand, ancient Eastern philosophy focuses on sitting in silence, becoming aware, controlling your mind, and understanding the world around you, to then be one with the world, not from a place of competition, but from a place of acceptance. The goal is not to conquer the world or oneself; it is to be one with it. Thus, Western philosophy is generally more attuned to the principles of capitalism and wealth accumulation. The East is just playing along because it must, in this world order created by the West.

In the world we live in today, driven by the forces of the

industrial revolution and colonialism, in large parts of Asia this means living in direct contradiction to what you are philosophically taught at home as the secret to happiness and what you are expected to accomplish professionally. This creates an atmosphere of looking at work, especially corporate work, more as a punishment or a duty to the family. What doesn't help is that often you are working for large corporations that are in your country simply to take advantage of you as cheap labor and your country as a large market, to then take profits back—a new form of colonization, if you will.

This usually ends up creating conditions for dutiful work that one despises but bears, for the lack of a better option. In places like India, concepts of karma and reincarnation make living a life of obligation and getting a "good job" for your family or community is seen as your dutiful karma. Thus, people go to work, often slogging it out for long hours with terrible commutes, and then look for fulfillment and reward through the lens of family life and community. This puts further obligatory pressures on relationships, especially intergenerational ones, with younger generations being considered more Western in thought and principle. This happens despite younger generations actively questioning the very Western systems that their parents gobbled up as gospel when escaping generations of financial hardship.

One example that demonstrates this is how Indians save. A Gen Xer or boomer in India would aspire to save at least 50 percent of their income, something everyone in my generation was told was essential. Gen-Xers and boomers were taught to despise materialistic or worldly pleasures, often because they could not be afforded and weren't readily available. They grew up in a socialistic India with a closed economy, until 1991, and often had just a couple of options to choose from, whether it was cars or airlines or soap or companies to work for. "Imported" was synonymous with "excellent" and still is a marketing gimmick in India. Indians choose to import unhealthy palm oil and wheat, despite there being healthier, cheaper domestic alternatives like ghee or grains like jowar and bajra.

Despite the availability of most major brands in India, it is still quite common for Indians to ask friends and families to get them products from abroad. I've been asked to carry everything from makeup and face washes to phones and drones while traveling back home. It just is so ingrained in people!

This socialistic attitude that despised materialistic pleasures changed spectacularly as India's economy transformed to a free market economy in 1991, with many other Asian economies also liberalizing in the 1990s. This was done because India had about 90 days of forex reserves left to pay its bills and needed International Monetary Fund (IMF) loans to avoid bankruptcy. That meant IMF conditions imposed a more open economy to allow companies to come in and set up shop in India. With the advent of television, it created the perfect conditions for global brands to flood India with the lures of consumerism—a young, aspirational nation with a rapidly rising middle class, hungry for goods that tapped into that aspiration.

In the following chart, CEIC Data shows India's gross savings rate as a percentage of GDP, which has been steadily falling since millennials joined the workforce.[9]

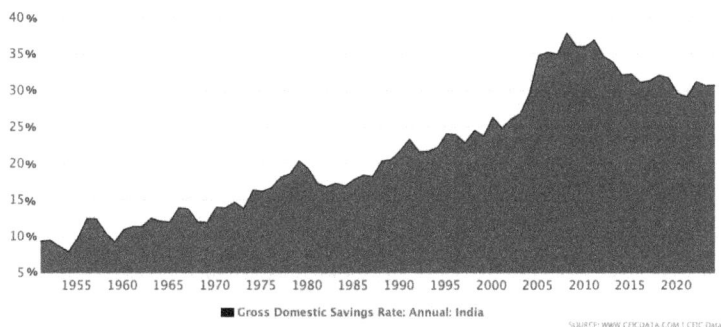

(Source: CEIC Data, "India Gross Savings Rate," 2022)

Till the early '90s, India generally went through a period of underwhelming economic growth with GDP per capita only growing from $90 per year in 1947 to $304 per year in 1991, which is about three times in 45 years. In the 34 years since my birth in 1991, India's per capita GDP has increased around nine times to $2,839 per year.[10]

Those early years, especially till the 1990s, were without banking access for many Indians. Thus, the savings rate does not account for a lot of the savings that were held in hard cash stashed in mattresses or India's favorite savings instrument, gold. Still, saving 15–25 percent as financial assets at a household per capita GDP of $100–$300 reflects a general propensity to save.

Those attitudes tended to persist, even with economic liberalization and an increasingly consumerist mindset in India. Credit was considered a bad word while I was growing up and my father shuddered at the thought of me having three credit cards and being invested in the stock market on his trip to America in 2019. He felt I was being extremely irresponsible.

In India, you see savings rates steadily increasing, to about 38 percent of GDP before the 2008 financial crisis. This period also coincided with GDP growth rates of over 7.5 percent in six of the nine years leading up to the financial crisis.[11] Thus, as Indian Gen Xers earned more, they saved a lot more. Increasing levels of access to banking and financial markets also enabled this.

After the 2008 financial crisis, with consumerism now well settled in India, the trend has been to save less and less, especially with millennials and now Gen Zers joining the workforce. Adoption of a more consumerist mindset with easier access to credit and "easy monthly installments" as a way of life with high rates of inflation has meant Indian households are stretched thinner.

According to research by the *Economic Times,* Indian households saw their financial assets shrink to 5.1 percent of GDP in FY2023, a 50-year low.[12] Household debt, as a percentage of the GDP, is also the highest it has been since independence in 1947, at 37.6 percent.[13]

What this trend tells us is that Asian economies have adopted increasingly Western ways of economic life, with family life still being driven by a more Eastern mindset. This creates a daily dichotomy at an individual level, creating a confused, uncommitted, collective consciousness. It is also apparent in the politics of today, with right-wing governments on the rise in Asia (think Modi, Duterte, etc.), which market an even more vehement rejection of "Western culture" while pushing people to buy more and work for large corporations, a consumption-driven capitalist economic model propagated by the West.

This contrarian life simply isn't designed for fulfillment and, in a nutshell, Asians are confused and torn between their

Eastern philosophy and the increasingly capitalistic setups they find themselves in.

Salaries in Asia also don't match up to the increasing demand placed on an individual by this consumerist mindset, creating sustained demand for more credit, a story far too common in places like the US.

Companies come to Asian markets for cheap labor—I joined Google at an entry-level job at about $300 a month in 2012, surprisingly competitive for Hyderabad, the sixth-largest city in India. The same job in the US would have cost the company at least $3,000 a month. Given the surplus labor in markets like India and most Asian economies, companies don't have an incentive to increase salaries and provide better working conditions or perks, in their home markets or in the markets they look to for cheap labor. Thus, the slog that feels like a punishment goes on. This is only increasing now through the gig economy where thousands of freelancers in Asian economies are doing everything on the cheap for Western economies.

Higher rates of inflation and constant currency devaluation means Indians on fixed incomes lose purchasing power, even as they earn more. When I was studying economics as a college student in 2008, one US dollar was worth about 40 Indian rupees. Today, the exchange rate is 86 Indian rupees to a dollar, effectively meaning the Indian rupee buys less than half of the dollar-value goods and services it did in 2008. Thus, even though India's economy grew significantly, the devaluation in currency meant Indians had to pay a lot more for imports.

This creates conditions for Indians to look for opportunities abroad, generally to the West. It also creates stereotypes like Indians and Chinese being extremely hardworking. Indians are often, rightly so, touted as the richest immigrant community in the US, mostly fueled by the wealth accumulation in the Silicon Valley boom and the migrations it drove.

However, large immigrant communities tend to cluster together abroad, creating "Little Indias" or "Chinatowns," trying to replicate some form of that important aspect of Eastern family life and community from back home. With their elders missing, that context-driven community life is often irreplaceable. Thus, many end up even more burned out, more guilt-ridden, with more money, but missing that broader context in their lives that truly enriched them.

Regional Attitudes Correlate to Burnout Rates

Group	Attitudes Toward Their Way of Life	Burnout/Happiness
Europeans	Most confident in their own attitudes and way of life; generally welfare-driven	Least burned out with smallest happiness gaps
Americans	Generally capitalistic and individualistic	Higher rates of burnout accompanied by lowering rates of happiness, as the deal gets worse
Asians	Conflicted between socialistic and capitalistic mindsets	Highest rates of burnout and lowest rates of happiness

While there is global recognition of such nuances in corporations, it is you who will have to recognize and adapt to your needs, based on your own unique journey and context. Wouldn't it make sense to aspire to work for companies more culturally aligned with what is important to you? I don't think any of us think about that in our job hunt when we evaluate whether we are a "culture fit."

If we do start to evaluate that, we know what to expect either way. And that awareness goes a long way in helping you set an empowering baseline for your corporate experience.

**CHOOSE PEOPLE,
NOT JOBS!**

**EMPOWER
YOURSELF WITH
VULNERABILITY**

Choose People, Not Jobs!

Most people might roll their eyes at how simplistic and first world this suggestion sounds. I admit, it is very easy to say that we should all strive to work with people we enjoy the company of. However, often, most of us aren't fortunate enough to make those choices. Most of us are in survival mode and simply need jobs to survive. Stay with me a minute, though.

Think back to a time you enjoyed a particular job. What did you specifically enjoy about it? It might be that there were exciting problems to solve. It might be that you enjoyed the direct impact your role had on the business. It might be that the team you worked with were a bunch of amazing people. You might have had an amazing relationship with your boss.

Whether you recognize it or not today, there were people within organizational structures enabling what you liked. You might have had a boss who shielded the worker bees to focus on doing the work that mattered. You might have had an executive who set in place a vision and a structure that drove clarity through the organization, and your work.

Everything within our social world is driven and enabled by people, whether you recognize that or not. Eventually, every single piece of work in the world is a collaboration.

This insight has guided me in my approach to building genuine, lasting relationships beyond time, roles, companies, and geography with colleagues past and present. It also helped me think about how I scour for opportunities through my network. I often had a negative, burdensome association with the word "networking" and how it is thrown around in the corporate world, almost always linked to mutual gainful back-scratching. It almost felt a bit cannibalistic to me—fostering a relationship with an eventual unknown gain in mind. It went against my genuine approach to life and relationships. But my thinking was misplaced.

So, I evolved to think of networking as building genuine friendships with interesting people I enjoyed interacting with. I don't force relationships with people who don't feel interesting to me just for the sake of networking. This doesn't mean I was rude or pushed people away. I just had the same attitude to networking I did with making friends. It was carefree, less burdensome, and it helped me build deeper, long-lasting relationships that enriched me through enduring friendships, long after our time working together ended. It made networking effortless. I might not have as large a network as someone who is masterful at networking for the sake of it, but I have a more reliable network, one that is more likely to come through for me. A higher qualitative ceiling, if you will.

And since a lot of my corporate network are truly friends,

I have been able to rely on their direction and advice fully, as I know they are like-minded people, aligned with my state of being. This helps me then generate quality leads and get genuine referrals from, not my network, but my friends.

In the US, there is an accepted idea around having a dual persona—a "work me" and a "life me." This is why US offices are usually empty at 5 p.m., with people rushing back to their lives. In places like India, it is common for people to be working late and hang out after, as these distinct personae aren't as pronounced.

The "work me" persona is usually a politically correct one, tailored for work. I never understood this contradiction, especially at companies like Google, which asked us "to bring our whole selves to work." This creates a burdensome, often awkward environment for work interactions, something that consumes five days of your week. Even when there are social events at work, they feel heavy, requiring a lot of effort (and alcohol) to get people to let loose, creating an obligatory environment around such events.

Thus, while choosing people, not jobs, might sound simplistic at face value, there is true value in building relationships that feel authentic to you at work, setting in motion a chain reaction that enables you to keep choosing people over jobs. Like in life, choose quality over quantity, and foster genuine relationships that last beyond the project you're working on today. Eventually, no matter what the project is, what you'll remember is the people you completed it with, and maybe what they made you feel.

Empower Yourself with Vulnerability

It is not uncommon for people struggling with mental health challenges to find ways to blame themselves. Low self-esteem is a common thread in people struggling with mental health that gets exacerbated when their lives are perceived as not going to plan. You may have convinced yourself that you're the only one who feels like completely blowing up your life, or your coworkers love everything about your company that you don't, or something is wrong with you if you aren't fitting in culturally at a company that is touted to have excellent work culture. Guess what, your suffering isn't unique or exceptional. And that's a good thing.

It is not just you who's burned out and spent. It might feel like you're in a unique, lonely place, but statistically that is simply not the case. There are many around you who are just looking for a moment of shared vulnerability, as no one else can relate better to the unique circumstances that make up your corporate context.

Most of us develop a protective external coating to help cope with the eccentricities of circumstance—one that helps us withdraw into whatever we define as our little protective cocoon. It helps us get through the mundaneness of life, be professional, and cope, regardless of our internal strife.

Whatever coating you developed—humor, ridicule, judgment, sadness—has helped you cope with the experiences life threw at you. So, take a moment to be thankful for it, even if you might despise it internally. Think of it as a partner you're making up with.

That cocoon naturally also leads us to our set ways. It leads to some of us convincing ourselves with thoughts like "Oh! Nobody will get it!" or "My life is way too complicated for anyone to understand" or "Who's interested in my sob story anyway?"

As stated earlier, in American offices in particular, this manifests through an adoption of a distinct "work me" persona, a cloak of professionalism, separate from the "real life me" whom friends and family meet after 6 p.m. This creates a general lack of vulnerability in work environments. This is something I felt distinctly when I moved to New York after working in India, Ireland, and Singapore.

Even in an overtly social company like Google, there were few in the office interested in truly becoming friends or hanging out in more casual settings. I ended up becoming good friends with many South Asians and Europeans in the New York office as they came from more casual, open working relationships too.

However, to genuinely do good work, especially as a team, there needs to be a mutual understanding of what the individuals who make the team are each bringing to the table. That understanding builds connection and can only manifest through a degree of shared vulnerability, something that shines through in successful teams, whether they are corporate or sports teams. I've been fortunate to work in teams through my career with empathetic leaders eager to create a degree of psychological safety within teams, an environment where opinions can be voiced without fear and people can admit their struggles. While there are always dynamic, interpersonal challenges that will pop up in professional environments, especially ones driven by deadlines, a baseline of psychological safety within teams will ensure feelings don't fester. In such teams, conflict resolves toward the genuine growth of the team rather than political bickering.

While most of us want to work in such teams, very few of us take steps toward nurturing a more vulnerable environment. While working in global teams, we always had challenges bonding across different time zones and market priorities. The Asia Pacific and China (APAC) team, for example, wouldn't really be able to bond with the Americas teams. This was a challenge for leadership toward creating truly global, collaborative work streams that could have cross-region impact. Having worked across all these regions, I was seen as someone who could act as a cultural bridge.

I thought deeply about how I could inspire my colleagues to be more engaged with their teammates across the seas, despite distinctly differing priorities and contexts. I also thought deeply about why I have enduring relationships with my colleagues, despite the distance and difference in priorities. My assessment was that it was because I fostered authentic relationships—friendships built through proactive vulnerability based on a shared human experience at work, but extending way beyond it. I didn't have a mental distinction between "work" and "life" me.

I truly cared about the experience people had working with me, learning from their experiences and always wanting them to understand why I had a differing opinion on a particular subject. While these seem to be simple things, you'd be surprised at how far they can go to create enduring working relationships.

I started presenting a quick module on "creating relationships over video conferencing (VC)." The one thing I stressed the most was the idea of "vulnerability creating vulnerability." Sharing something that makes you feel vulnerable—from anything as small as your fear of spiders to feeling burned out at work can go a long way in helping someone else open up to you in return.

You would be surprised to learn how similarly people feel and experience the world, especially in the little, niche worlds companies create within themselves, with their own laws, acronyms, and ways of being. Only with the acknowledgment of the similarities of our collective experience can we begin to heal and create a support system for us, and everyone around us.

Your vulnerability to share even a little bit will empower you and everyone around you to find the true strength within to redefine your relationship with your work, your colleagues, and, most importantly, with your "work me." This will help create a collective sense of suffering and empowerment, across people who deeply relate to the unique corporate context they find themselves in.

PART THREE

THE INNER CHILD THAT CONTROLS YOU

THE MENTAL TOLL OF THE
BURNOUT HIGHWAY

THE DEMONIZATION OF REST

A DECLINE OF THE COLLECTIVE

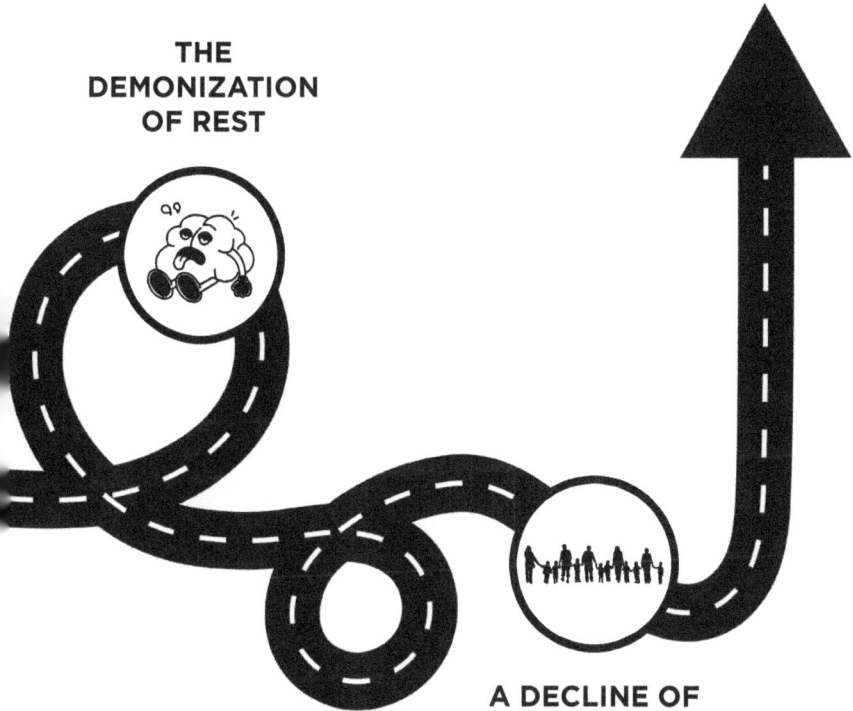

CHAPTER 7

The Inner Child That Controls You

We may not want to admit or like it, but we all have our natural vibrations that serve as our default states. Everything in the universe does. Whether you describe it as energy, vibes, alignment of chakras, or the many other ways humans convey the same idea, people have baseline energies. Some people have to be the chirpiest in the room; others want to sit in a corner and observe everyone. Some of us are described as grumpy, some happy, some stoic, some distant. Eventually, we are all our energy, individually and collectively.

This baseline energy forms the basis of our personality and thus the basis of everything we experience. These default states govern our interpretation of various experiences and how we respond to situations. And when our baseline energies are

based in anxiety or fear, we gravitate toward reductive outcomes, professionally and personally.

While there is debate, it is commonly agreed upon by experts
that children tend to develop core personality traits before the
age of five. While our personalities evolve through childhood,
and even into adulthood, foundational traits usually stand the
test of time.

In the largest study of its kind I could find online, Professor
Avshalom Caspi of King's College London and the University of
Wisconsin conducted a study over a 23-year period with 1,000
three-year-olds in Dunedin, New Zealand, that rated each child
across 22 characteristics or personality traits.[1] It began in 1970,
and researchers were able to observe 96 percent of the children
through their childhood up until they were 26 years old, con-
ducting health exams and interviews. The researchers also had
an "informant," someone who knew the participant well, who
filled out a questionnaire describing the person's personality at
26. Longitudinal studies like this one are rare, as they are expensive and complex to conduct.

The researchers clustered the 22 personality traits into five
types of children or personalities: well adjusted, confident,
inhibited, reserved, and uncontrolled (impulsive, restless, and
distracted).

The study found that characteristics the children exhib-
ited at age three were evident as the children reached age 18.
However, these traits continued to be obvious even at 26,
after many major life events like full-time jobs, weddings,
and parenthood. "Confident" children grew up to score low
on self-control and be uninhibited, the chirpiest ones in the
room. "Inhibited" children on the other hand showed high

levels of constraint as an adult and scored low on positive emotional attitude.

While this has many implications on parenting and the need for early behavioral interventions in education programs, it also has an obvious implication on the person's perception of life itself, as a child and, therefore, as an adult.

This doesn't mean that we can't overcome problematic behaviors like anger or aggression, for example. It just means that our foundational personality was coded into us at a time we don't even consciously remember, at our most vulnerable, by the people around us and that early context of our lives. And fighting those personality traits means fighting your own subconscious default states—states that were encoded into us through unique circumstances and genetic makeup.

What drives early childhood personality is obviously a combination of factors, but it is generally agreed upon in psychology that there are three broad influences—heredity, environment, and situation.

What You Got from the Ones Who Brought You into This World

Heredity is basically the weird concoction of genes that your parents gave you, a cocktail of the ones they got. It is why you look like them, act like them, and, many times, feel like them. Eventually, it is impossible to escape where you came from, no matter how hard you try. Take it from someone who has actively tried escaping my roots, chomping at the bit for another move, when the last one didn't fulfill me as much as I expected it to.

In mental health diagnoses, there is an emphasis on mental illnesses in family history. That is because, for some of us, no matter what we do, our genetic makeup is a bit grumpy. No amount of toxic positivity will fix that, but an awareness of traits you dislike within your parents/family can make parts of yourself that you dislike a bit friendlier. You can then approach those traits with curiosity, enabling you to make positive behavioral changes.

For me, recognizing and calling out anxiety in my mother and uncle made me articulate and cope with my own struggles with overthinking and anxiety that had ever plagued my existence. Dealing with it professionally has also helped me coach my mother with tools to cope with her constant anxiety, since going to therapy in semi-urban, tier-3 India is basically still a nonexistent concept. There isn't much you can do to change these traits and you're likely to be like your parents. Don't fight it, but understand it, become aware of it, and optimize for it.

The Environment You Grew Up in and the Cards You Were Handed

Environment refers to the nurturing aspect of our lives. It relates to where we live and grow up, which obviously plays a huge role in the story of our lives. The home we grow up in, the school we go to, the languages we speak, the cultural norms we adhere to all have a profound impact on our personalities. If you grew up in a family where nobody really talked at dinner, it'll feel awkward to go to a dinner where everyone in the family speaks over one another.

That similar environment or context subsequent generations continue to nurture is the basis of generational wealth,
poverty, and personality being passed on from generation to
generation. This bit is easier to escape physically as an adult,
since your physical environment is something you can control
to an extent. However, the traits that you formed due to the
environment of your early childhood will follow you, no matter where you go.

Your environment also goes a long way in setting your mindset toward many things in life—how you think of money, what
constitutes a good life, how many rules you follow, and so on.
Think about the environment you grew up in. Was money tight
at home when you grew up? Did your parents constantly fight?
Did the society you grew up in encourage certain rash behaviors? Think of some of the problematic behaviors or mental
patterns you are trying to rid yourself of and how your early
environment might have framed that default state.

As someone who grew up in India and then experienced
such different environments through the course of my life
experiences, I started noticing how starkly behaviors change
just by being in another environment. For example, one thing
that I hated growing up in India was littering and the general lack of civic sense with regards to public cleanliness and
hygiene. The same people who would cut a ticket queue or
throw trash out of their cars in India would suddenly transform into model citizens while traveling abroad, because their
environment had changed.

Situations refer to everything that happens to us in our lives
that frames us. In our early childhood, we could have been
deeply influenced by the death of a loved one or economic

hardships in the family or a political conflict that affected the environment we lived within.

Thus, heredity is something that you literally just have to live with, while your environment and situations are more external and evolve as the context of your life changes. Situations are closely linked to your environment, and thus the easiest way to change your situation is usually changing your environment.

Finding Awareness of What Makes You, You

There is no way of telling whether heredity, environment, or situations influence personality traits the most. It likely depends on everyone's own context and story. However, everyone should find an awareness of their own default states that they formed long ago. Triggers and responses that subconsciously control millions of neurons within you are dictating your experience of life itself.

While there are many reasons why the environment and situations of children born in developed nations give them a better shot at life than those born in developing or underdeveloped countries, being born in a more prosperous economic environment is paramount. That enables everything from a better school to better air to breathe, the ability to access a library and better nutrition, all foundationally important to being a functional human being.

Having your basic physiological needs met and seeing others around you have their basic needs met gives a child a sense of security that is critical to finding psychological safety. It is natural that a child who grew up with anxious parents stressed out about money will also harbor those fears well into adulthood. The challenge many burned-out individuals face is ridding themselves of the fears and protections they perceive they need, even after they are in comfortable situations.

Having spent some time in the northern suburbs of Chicago, getting to know where my wife grew up, I've witnessed firsthand the role of the environment in our respective upbringings. While we are similarly anxious people, the fears we harbor are quite different—I worry about existential stuff, and she worries about everything beyond existential stuff. And if a combination of heredity, environment, and situations made you fear-driven, you are likely to lead with fear in your career.

The Role of Fear in Corporate Careers

Fear is a big driver for all of us. Fear plays a positive role in our lives; it helps us make wise decisions. It has played an important role in evolution and helped us gauge situational fight-or-flight responses. However, fear also stifles us when we don't need to make a wise decision, when we can afford to lead with joy, contentment, and fulfillment instead.

A default state entrenched in fear enables you to survive, not thrive.

While the fears we choose to live by can be driven by a combination of heredity, environment, and situations, they play a big role in our corporate careers, and you could argue people who lead more with fear gravitate toward the stability of a long-term corporate career, something I did for over a decade.

The role fear plays in careers is not well understood and needs to be studied in detail. A 2023 survey by Love Leadership and First & First Consulting with over 2,000 managers aged 24–54 years across 50 companies in the US, UK, and Australia sought to try to answer this question from a corporate perspective: "Are you driven by fear?"[2]

They did not ask the question directly, however. In surveys, people don't tend to speak truthfully and additionally most people don't even tend to be that aware of their feelings. Thus, they asked questions around fear-based sentiments and tendencies of fear-based management.

Fear-based sentiments include aggression, avoidance, suspicion, and blame. Tendencies of fear-based management include recurring feelings of anxiety, a desire to micromanage, feelings of impostor syndrome, complacency, and an unwillingness to receive feedback.

What the survey found was that a third of the managers who responded were driven by fear. Additionally, they found that 40 percent of fear-driven managers believed that stress could be used to harness positive performance objectives. In the US, the proportion of fear-based managers was 36 percent, a bit higher than the overall average of 33 percent.[3]

While there may be many negative outcomes, including negative financial outcomes for the company with fear-based leadership, fear is part of the fabric of the corporate ladder. It is what keeps you in jobs you hate or keeps you from alternate paths you pine to explore. It is natural to feel that the opportunity cost of doing something else is way too high.

When you were a child and anyone asked what you would be when you grew up, what did you say? I don't think your answer would be a corporate leader or CEO. Skills associated with being a C-level executive aren't comprehensible at that age. A kid could idolize a CEO and want to be like that person, but that is a different thing altogether. That's because nobody grows up with a desire to imbibe skills that corporate leaders require, such as the ability to navigate a political environment, be good at presenting, run efficient workflows, make people feel heard, or resolve conflicts.

That is because these are secondary, supporting skills that come naturally to some and not so naturally to others. Moreover, these skills support a primary skill that gives us fulfillment when we engage with it. The primary skill, which is the answer kids give, would be something like astronaut, writer, pilot, footballer, fashion designer, politician, photographer, painter, and so on. You simply don't grow up with the desire of being a corporate leader as that isn't a primary skill. And as a kid, you need to feel engaged and immersed in a skill to learn. We often forget that as adults.

If you, as a young adult, focus on a professional path through a primary skill you think you have a knack for, it is important to be able to monetize that as a business or service. Naturally, if your skill requires a large canvas—for example, a fashion designer with your own clothing company, the secondary skills of an effective corporate leader will help you. If you don't have those secondary skills of effectively managing a team, aligning priorities of various departments, satisfying investors, and everything else that comes with running a large clothing company, the primary skill that got you there in the first place might start to feel like a chore.

Earlier, we examined how corporate structures create incentives for linear paths, where you get more and more boxed into a particular process or area of expertise, with the only obvious path usually being managerial roles within that path. This is especially true for people who have demonstrated proficiency in a process or area of expertise. New managers who can't adapt to stepping away from individual task-based responsibilities they might have enjoyed or felt engaged with, to managerial ones, struggle with some secondary skills that corporate management demands. They end up as fear-driven managers.

And what corporate management demands is a lot of those soft skills with a hard outer casing, one that can take a lot of shit being thrown at it! For me, as I progressed through my corporate career, I felt this at every stage, as managerial elements were added to my jobs.

When I was in a sales support job, for example, it wasn't enough that I was driving incremental performance for my client's advertising. I had to be introduced as the expert to the client and make them feel like they were getting something extraordinary in the form of me.

When I was in a direct sales role, it wasn't enough that I was delivering on our revenue targets while delivering on the client's media efficiency goals. I had to be the bridge between various points of client leadership to our internal leadership, which involved endlessly boastful emails after a simple meeting, a newsletter nobody read but was considered important, unnecessary client events, being a slave to my inbox, and so on.

When I was in a research role, it wasn't enough that I was driving every project goal that was given to me on paper and I was told was "business critical." I had to also satisfy a certain intangible, perception-based goal about how leaders across various organizations within the company were perceiving our work. And that perception was based on the perception of my boss's perception of those leaders' perceptions, based on many micro interactions, direct and indirect. See the challenges with seeking fulfillment in a cluster of unconfirmed, secondhand perceptions?

Yet, I enjoyed the nuts and bolts of most of these jobs. I enjoyed understanding the intricacies of the Google Ads algorithm to give my clients tangible media performance gains. I loved setting up complex media measurement studies to understand media channels in different ways across the globe, tweaking studies to market nuances. What engaged me most was behavioral research at Google's Human Truths team, plagued with a fascinating new problem about human behavior every few months, finding answers in innovative methodologies, in a dataset that was a continuous time stamp of humanity. That is the bit I miss the most from my work at Google.

When I was asked to manage the Emerging Markets division of Google Human Truths, I was told that it was business imperative that we had a physical team in the Asia Pacific and China region, and that I was the only person who had the skills to deliver it. I was persuaded, with an eye-watering expat package, and was even granted an extremely generous working situation driven by COVID, where I got to use Mumbai as a base for a year while setting up a team in Singapore.

However, I always feared the perils of the poor corporate structure and incentives we worked within—being a cutting-edge research team within a sales organization, the furthest from revenue. And when the winds changed, as they rapidly do in the corporate world, all I was left with were endless responsibilities to prove that we were in fact needed in APAC, while pretending to my team that all was rosy. The incentives that were used to persuade me to come and deliver a "critical business need" were now pitfalls of a need that was starting to be perceived as more of a luxurious desire of a particular VP, who left for another organization.

Thus, all I was doing was trying to be the meat in a sandwich between my team and an insecure set of superiors, driven by fear. Priorities would constantly shift based on the winds and leaders of the day and I was left with absolutely nothing that engaged me; the work was taken away and replaced by a political chess match.

This experience is far too common for far too many corporate managers. And based on my experience of the corporate world, I believe there are far more than 33 percent of corporate managers who are driven by fear.

Fear is embedded in the fabric of the corporate ladder, and when fear takes over, it is natural to lose connection with your work. Ever notice a striker in soccer struggling with their confidence and feeling like they'll never be able to score a goal again? Something they trained for and loved all their life feels like their least favorite chore. It feels like they're disconnected from the game and can't operate in a childlike, autopilot mode anymore. That's fear. Imagine if Cristiano Ronaldo or Lionel Messi or Tiger Woods constantly focused on their fears rather than their connection with their sport. Would they be among the greatest athletes the world has ever known, or just chokers?

Fear of Losing Out

Corporate work has monetarily guaranteed a better life for many of its participants for over a century now. While that guarantee is becoming less secure, it still holds true for a top-tier corporate career.

However, it is natural that beyond a certain level of corporate growth, the fear of losing that kind of financial stability takes over, a fear of missing this "open goal" you sacrificed so much to attain.

In the same 2023 survey by Love Leadership and First & First Consulting cited earlier, they also found that the average salary of fear-driven managers was about $119,000 a year.[4] So, that seems to be the number where fear takes over in your corporate journey. And that makes sense as that is a number that most feel begins to enable a comfortable life in the US. You often don't hear of entry-level employees or the CEOs being burned out. The CEOs simply have more resources and power to deal with it, even if they are burned out. As we discussed in an earlier chapter, burnout is usually most prevalent in the middle—of organizations, of careers, of life itself.

No one likes to live in that exhausted state. Yet, the demands of our lives force us to stay in jobs that literally exhaust us. The continuing layoffs of 2023–2025 and the advent of AI have only heightened this sense of fear in corporate workers, especially higher-paid and mid-level employees with bleaker prospects in the job market. People who are in such jobs are always looking over their shoulders. People who have been laid off are faced with the fear of making it in the hardest job market in the history of America, one where being a LinkedIn influencer will hold you in better stead than being a master at your subject matter. I know many people struggling with their fear in both states.

For a top-tier corporate worker today and in the next few

decades, this fear will only get worse, with Sundar Pichai, the CEO of Google, recently saying that AI could be "more profound than fire."[5] It is not hard to imagine a world where humans will be working for AI. It will happen soon enough. Even laws aren't written for the possibilities and outcomes AI is driving already from the realm of capital market transactions, privacy, and so on.

In such an environment, it is natural that anyone who is in fear of navigating change and uncertainty will feel crippled. It is thus no surprise that the layoffs of the last couple of years have been severely targeted at middle management, the most fear-driven group in the corporate world and the most easily replaceable by AI.

Thus, especially as a mid-level employee today, it is harder to grow vertically as organizations get leaner, it is less financially rewarding with lower job security, and you are faced with a vastly more political environment, both within organizations and in the job market. If you've not engaged with the skills that might hold you in good stead to resurrect your personal economy, you will struggle with even more fear, anxiety, and burnout.

The only way out of this fear-driven cycle is engaging with the primary skills that brought you true joy and engaged you, finding an awareness of the drivers of that inner child that still controls you. While that may sound like "no shit" advice, be honest with yourself and conduct an audit of how many things you engage with professionally that give you joy. If it is fewer than three a week, you need to find engagement through other means.

And today, that is very easy to do through the internet economy. If you want to be a rock tumbler, you can find others who are rock tumblers. And once you do, being a rock tumbler, on the side, doesn't seem as crazy. So, if you can't quit your job, find three things a week you can engage with and see where that path takes you. This will help you move from a fearful to an engaged mindset, something that will forge a new dawn.

CHAPTER 8

The Demonization of Rest

R est, or a stable state of mental emptiness, doesn't come easy to human beings. Meditation and mindfulness focus on clearing your mind, bringing you back from a racing mind full of thoughts to a restful one. This restlessness, however, has formed the basis of our remarkable progress and achievement as a species. Eventually, a restful restlessness, a state of neutrality, is what brings optimal performance. A pro golfer, for example, needs to have a clear, restful mind to not choke on or unnecessarily muscle a drive. However, they also need a degree of restlessness toward the game to continue to get better.

Hard Work vs. Fulfilling Work

As a society, we've generally romanticized the feeling of busy-ness and the value of hard work at the expense of rest, especially since the industrial revolution. Just look at all the advice summarized as "I work more hours than everyone else" across the "manosphere." Capitalism and vocationalism have played a prime role in pushing this narrative, and we've often failed to make the distinction between how rewarding hard work can be when working on something that we connect with versus hard work for the sake of work or to make a living.

In his 2010 book *The Burnout Society,* often considered a seminal piece of writing on burnout, Byung-Chul Han talks about how we live in an "achievement society."[1] The basis of that achievement society is a feeling of restlessness, which embeds in us this idea that you should never feel content, always trying to hit a new level of achievement, a new bottom line, a new set of skills, and so on.

I grew up in a culture that taught me to take to heart adages like "work is worship" or "idle mind, devil's workshop." In Hindi, there is the adage "aaram haraam hai," which literally translates to "rest is forbidden or bad." My father's identity is linked to the work he does, and he does not have the ability to sit with himself, even at 66. His solution to every emotional challenge has been to just get busy. He studied to be an electrical engineer but has practiced, through his businesses, being a civil engineer, hotelier, builder, accountant, lawyer, copywriter, marketing manager, and many other things.

To me, it has been both admirable and disgusting to see the breadth of his knowledge and the hours of work he can still put in. It wasn't uncommon for me as a child to go to bed at around 11 p.m. and see my father at his desk when I woke up at 7 a.m., after yet another "all-nighter," something he still pulls off, even at this age! He also believes that working that hard is his moral responsibility and duty to his family.

My mother, though, is a bit more balanced in her attitude to work. She was a teacher, which meant her hours were confined to the 8 a.m. to 3 p.m. school window and she had two to three months of vacation a year. Also artistically inclined, she had that time to paint and write because of her school schedule. Thus, I ended up a cocktail, often feeling guilty for not wanting to work as hard as my father, unless it was on something that truly engaged or fulfilled me—which, as I discussed earlier, was something I did not generally find through my corporate career.

While hard work is a virtue, the romanticization of hard work, rather than the romanticization of fulfilling work, is problematic. Hard work is achieved easily via a fulfilling connection. Since the rise of vocationalism and path-based education, coupled with the increased cost and the need for higher education, work has been increasingly linked to the need to not make a living doing something that fulfills you, but to make a living to justify the paths taken early on. While most of us try to make that marriage early on in our career, it is a hard endeavor in the way the world is set up.

The Obsession with Presenteeism

The industrial revolution brought with it a need and obsession with "employee presenteeism." Factory owners needed workers to turn up every day, for a certain number of hours, executing a certain set of menial tasks a certain number of times. Presenteeism as a factory worker was a basic requirement for promotion to supervisor, manager, and so on, and such rewards incentivized presenteeism for all factory workers. Remnants of this practice continue to this day in the corporate

world—often in the name of creating a culture or collaboration—through badging in, badging out, the generally accepted
nine-to-five workday, and corporate timesheets. Presenteeism
also means we accept long commutes and long workdays, often
at the expense of rest.

The struggles after the COVID pandemic across the world
to get "back to the office" after working remotely show that
most of us never really wanted to sign up for presenteeism.
However, returning to a physical location for work is deemed
as demonstrating a seriousness toward work. As a result, for
people who still work remotely or on a hybrid schedule, there
has been a surge in talk about ways corporate managers can
track remote workers as "being at work." And because every
action elicits an equal and opposite reaction, social media is
flooded with ways to trick your boss and not appear "idle"
on work platforms.

We have ended up in this place where there is this constant
tension around shirking. But why is most of the corporate
world so prone to shirking and the ones who manage corporate workers so bent on ensuring people don't shirk? The
wide prevalence of shirking and the need to solve it within
corporate life itself demonstrates the general lack of connection we've just collectively accepted as "part of the job." Even
with remote work, there are forced procedural collaborations
that demand presenteeism. Additionally, managers and executives continue the push for presenteeism to justify their own
jobs and need for supervision. The need for and the strict
implementation of presenteeism, along with the unquestioning attitudes of boomers, Gen Xers, and, generally, millennials
too, brought such outcomes.

The Gift of Restlessness

To get a sense of how much of our attention technology demands, in addition to just checking in with yourself on days with too much smartphone time, all you must do is look at some statistics. The 2025 *State of Mobile Report* by Sensor Tower (formerly App Annie and data.ai), for instance, shows that the average person spent 13 minutes every waking hour on their smartphone in 2024. That is over a fifth of humanity's time awake! Consumers downloaded about 258,000 apps per minute globally, and we collectively spent 3 trillion hours on social media apps in 2024.[2]

These statistics are mind-boggling and, for me, show the number of mental tasks we've outsourced to our smartphones and the apps on them. Also, it emphasizes the mental energy and time we now devote to tech. I've outsourced my memory to Google Photos and Contacts and spend a lot of my free time on social media or YouTube. Moreover, everyone now needs an online presence in addition to doing whatever they do professionally. What was marketed as free to us was in fact never free, if you truly believe that time is money, that is. Today, we could say "time and data are money." This transformation we've made as humans to copying our lives on the cloud is less than a decade old.

What this time spent looking down into our phones has taken away from us is interactions with others and a decline in the favorite pastime for humans through most of our history: reading. In his book *Stolen Focus: Why You Can't Pay Attention—and How to Think Deeply Again,* Johann Hari delves deep into the many reasons why we have lost the ability to focus and how we've crippled our flow states. Flow state is an effortless state of deep absorption and concentration—an "in the zone" mental configuration. Like many counterintuitive things in the world, flow states are hard to attain deliberately and come easily during activities like walking or driving or in nature, when your brain doesn't consciously need to control the body, and there is room for wandering and involuntary attention.

Prime reasons for the crippling of our flow states include the distractions we've built into our lives through intrusive and invasive tech, impending pings, and notifications that limit our minds' ability to just be bored and wander.

These distractions are so deeply ingrained in how the world functions that we don't consciously recognize how long they impact us for. Every single time you go to a store, physical or online, you are asked for a way to contact you. This is now true for any website or app, too. You don't interact with a brand anymore. You sign up for a lifetime of emails, texts, calls, and mail. Technology has enabled such intrusive marketing to become the norm.

All this creates not a state of rest, but a state of excessive restlessness. As we get more inundated with technology, with server space getting cheaper and tech companies making provisions to essentially copy our lives online, monetizing it one strip of data at a time, this restlessness will only get worse. Notice the restlessness you feel on days when you've had a little too much social media and the calmness you feel on days you've kept away.

Technology, especially the way it is designed today, is meant to monetize your attention, measured by time spent on platforms. As a part of sales teams at Google, we commissioned extensive studies to prove that people spent more time on our platforms than on other platforms. Additionally, advertisers were interested in how much of that time was attentive, and we measured that through a metric called "viewability." More than 80 percent of Alphabet's estimated $100 billion revenue per year still comes through advertising,[3] essentially by monetizing time and attention on their platforms.

If you think back to the early eras of the internet in the late '90s and through the 2000s, remember scrolling and reaching the end of a page and then having to click to go to the next page? In 2006, Aza Raskin designed what we now call the "infinite scroll." He has since built a career out of the regret for his own invention and currently runs the Center for Humane Technology. You can watch the documentary *The Social Dilemma* on Netflix to learn more about his regret.[4]

Infinite scrolling, along with the move toward algorithmic feeds in 2011, rather than chronological ones, is what keeps you on a page endlessly, increasing viewability and ad impressions. This means more ads, more time spent, and, thus, more revenue. Infinite scroll is now a standard design practice. Thus, technology today is designed to make you spend as much time as possible on it rather than solve your need, distracting you from everything else around you in the real, natural world, everything that may give you fulfillment.

This is because algorithmic feeds and infinite scrolling work through the activation of dopamine receptors in our brains. This is the same reaction your brain has when it is on stimulant drugs like cocaine or ecstasy. Essentially, dopamine gets you charged up and gears you up for action. You also need more of the drug for a similar dopamine hit, and the higher the levels of dopamine, the harder the drop when you cut that supply off.

This is why you feel exhaustion while endlessly scrolling, but you continue to do it anyway.

Think back to your last vacation where you might have made plans on completely switching off and resting up. However, you ended up going to every single spot recommended by the many travel influencers on Instagram or TikTok. And then, you spent a bunch of time creating stories or posts about it. And then, on the last day of your vacation, you felt even more tired than before. Ever feel like you have lost the ability to rest? You and most of humanity have!

This is only getting worse, even though tech companies are making you believe that it is getting better. Like most things anti–big corporations, the EU has been a flag bearer for privacy laws, launching General Data Privacy Regulation (GDPR), which came fully into effect in 2018 and made it harder for companies to track users online through cookies. It is because of GDPR that you need to consent to cookies and have the option to reject all cookies every time you visit a website.

Because technology is so intrusive, more of us now are starting to value privacy and acknowledging the uncomfortable truth that our devices are listening to us, and we may have given up too much of ourselves. However, most of us are hooked, needing our next dopamine hit.

On the back of that privacy wave in Europe, tech companies, as corporations often do, tried to get ahead of the narrative. Apple launched the ability to "turn off tracking" on their iPhones in 2020 and Google has also launched something similar on Google Chrome and Android. They've also created modes in phones like "Do Not Disturb" or screen modes that reduce the amount of blue light. Smart tech companies are now marketing themselves as responsible advocates of privacy and giving you the illusion of control, after having set the world up for intrusion and restlessness.

Be Careful about What Is Marketed as a Choice

Privacy is being marketed as an empowered choice to the consumer, as something like this always ends up being marketed when regulatory pressures arise. That narrative, one used by corporations for centuries, creates the illusion of choice in what is increasingly a choiceless world. You simply do not have a choice to complete certain tasks without apps or digital touchpoints today, from buzzing someone into your apartment to accessing your health records. It also puts the onus on the individual—a capitalistic favorite! If you read the terms and conditions you said yes to, to even install a smartphone app, your eyes would pop.

Tech companies are offering ad-free environments because they have, to an extent, found another business model: subscriptions. Essentially, if you want an ad-free, less intrusive experience, commit to paying them more every month. I believe this is a bit more positive, but subscriptions are just about priced at a point where most of us are disincentivized to pay for it and just go with the ads. That is because these companies still need the advertising revenue, as subscription revenue is unlikely to catch up with the cash cows that are ads, especially with the decline of traditional media channels like print, radio, and TV.

Also, what the subscription model creates is a lack of ownership for the individual. If you bought a record or a VCR or a cassette or a CD of an album, you owned that. Today, through subscriptions, you don't own anything and are constantly paying for everything; for example, you are paying for all the music you may or may not consume on Spotify or Apple Music. This is incentivizing and making people used to choiceless consumption behaviors, even across things like music and cinema.

Another way tech companies are now bringing us to spend more time with them is through augmented reality (AR), virtual reality (VR), and AI. Apple, in 2023, through its headset Apple Vision Pro, showcased the concept of spatial computing, which aims at creating a oneness between human and computer to usher in a new age of personal computing. In its press release, Apple says that any space can be transformed into what feels like a 100-foot movie theater screen. This is true for the various solutions that Meta, Google, and so on are trying to build through concepts like the Metaverse.

Thus, the next age of computing is designed to make you and the computer truly one, a cyborg, by blurring the boundaries between the physical and the virtual, between human and artificial intelligence. Technology is moving from being intrusive toward being immersive, from monetizing your time to monetizing your physical space and your very existence.

What Gen Z and Their Tech Inundation Can Teach Us about Burnout

While Gen Z seems to be the most empathetic generation yet, it also seems the most exhausted and burned out, even before long years at work. There seems to be a sense of dread about the future among young people. While the industrial revolution, in a sense, demonized rest and romanticized hard work through presenteeism, Gen Z is actively fighting that. Despite that, they are more acutely aware of and affected by mental health challenges.

In the US, in 2022, a survey by McKinsey found that 55 percent of Gen Zers have received a mental health diagnosis or treatment.[5] There might be a myriad of reasons behind that, but we simply cannot ignore the fact that this is the first generation that has grown up with the internet and the intrusive technology that we now believe is a part of our sustenance. Instagram, for example, launched in 2010, when Gen Zers would have been between 8 and 13 years old.

Generationally speaking, a 2023 survey by Pew Research of 5,000-plus Americans showed that two-thirds of Americans over 65 were extremely satisfied with their jobs, and more than 50 percent of those aged 30–64 were satisfied. However, only 44 percent of those aged 18–29 indicated they were satisfied with their jobs.[6] Thus, more young people (i.e., Gen Zers) are looking at the glass as half-empty and beginning to question this narrative that demands long years of hard work for a slow and steady reward.

The labor force participation rate for Gen Z, according to the Bureau of Labor Statistics and *The Economist,* is the lowest at about 71 percent, while Gen Xers and millennials at the same age (20–24 years) were at 78 percent and 75 percent, respectively.[7]

Additionally, many Gen Zers do not see work as a core part of their identity. According to March 2023 Deloitte research in the US, 61 percent of Gen Zers already in the workforce thought of work as a core part of their identity as opposed to 86 percent of their bosses.[8] This tension bodes well for the future of empathy and mental health at work, but at this stage, it is creating tensions. In an April 2023 survey by ResumeBuilder.com, 74 percent of managers and business leaders said that they find "Gen Z more difficult to work with than other generations."[9] As someone who has only managed Gen Zers, I can vouch for the fact that their generational expectations and attitudes differ greatly from millennials'.

Helping young people navigate this uncharted turn in the economy is something that I believe is critical for the success of the world, and this economic model. Through my efforts at WideWorldView.com, I've tried to make this the mission of my coaching and consulting work.

You can't argue against the fact that the inundation of technology has hit Gen Zers from a very young age. Their comfort in online spaces, even more than in person, is quite apparent. For a millennial like me, it is unthinkable to call a friend without texting them first. Gen Zers, on the other hand, go about their lives, performing menial tasks, while on FaceTime with their friends. They practically live online.

This constancy of technology in our lives has created a more exhausted world, one where we are unable to focus on and enjoy anything, neither work nor rest. Instagram was launched in October 2010. Think back to the world before that (or even before social media at all). How did you spend your time?

I, for one, had the time and energy to call my friends, without needing to text them before. I also had the time, focus, and energy to read two whole newspapers on my two-hour-long commute in Mumbai. I waited for a football or a cricket match, exactly when it was being shown on TV, discussing it with friends in person through the week. If I missed it, I would then wait for the highlights, again at a specific time.

This nothingness in between things we looked forward to meant we had the time to be bored and let our minds wander. The fact that we felt bored a lot also made the event more important and anticipated. So, we looked forward to things more. Today, we check our phones hundreds of times a day, able to access anything on demand, and still feel bored, which also creates a subconscious cycle of guilt, apathy, and defeatism.

The Importance of Mental Wandering

What a sense of boredom or mental emptiness creates is space for wandering. That wandering helps us create new neural connections in our brains that help us make sense of unrelated things. It is when creativity occurs. If you've ever noticed yourself having more creative thoughts when you are on a walk or just doing nothing that you need to actively focus on, there is an explanation for that.

As humans, we have two types of attention states—voluntary and involuntary. Voluntary attention, as the name suggests, is the conscious attention we devote to a task or a problem. This is the state we are in when we are actively trying to focus on something, practice, or execute.

While voluntary attention is often responsible for a lot of the day-to-day progress we see in the world, involuntary attention is the fuel keeping the fire of voluntary attention burning. Often, after a few long weeks or months, when we feel like we need a break from work, it is our mind telling us that it has run out of its voluntary attention supplies. It needs to be renewed through involuntary attention.

Involuntary attention is the type of attention that does not require active effort, something that draws you in involuntarily, without requiring effort, and it helps you relax. Involuntary attention is most easily achieved in nature. Picture the last time you were in nature, whether it was by a lake, on the beach, in a forest, or atop a mountain.

Do you remember being effortlessly drawn to the sound of a gushing stream or the waves crashing onto the beach? Do you remember noticing a butterfly emerge from behind a tree or the faintly different hues in a forest? Do you remember noticing how crisp the mountain air felt or a difference in the color of the sky?

If you can't remember the last time you were in nature, go out in nature and notice when any of that happens. That is involuntary attention, attention that makes you feel restful and fuels voluntary attention. It is why doctors have begun prescribing nature walks for depression.

These are all things that we are drawn to and have in abundance around us. However, we as a species have stopped being in nature, or just generally outside, as much as we always were throughout the 300,000 years of *Homo sapiens* existence. Being in nature is the best way to recharge, and to recharge, we need to allow our minds to wander, achieving involuntary attention.

The Instant Gratification Treadmill

What social media, email, the internet, and technology generally have created is a constant, false sense of urgency, for both effort and reward. The scope for virality, instant fame, and the instantaneous nature of communication has meant that we, as a species, have less patience to dedicate ourselves to master something, by learning the many facets of making any endeavor successful. This is something we, as a human race, have never been accustomed to, or built for, until the age of the internet demanded this instantaneousness from us.

This desire for instant reward is in all of us. I, for one, was an avid blogger through the 2010s, wanting to share perspective on what I thought were my own unique experiences. I wrote many posts, tried a few different platforms, fueled by wanting to write but also wanting to go viral. However, I just expected that sharing my blog to the 1,000 or so people on my social media would be good enough to achieve that virality. In fact, blogging requires a lot of work, in relation to the type of content you are putting out there, the search engine optimization strategies, collaborations with other bloggers or publications, and so on. This is what I learned as I set up Mountains and Mahals with my wife.

If you've ever found yourself constantly checking your last Instagram post for likes, it is the same psychological process. Now, this desire for instant gratification has always been there for us humans. The internet has just delivered that en masse. Had I been setting up a newspaper or a magazine, I wouldn't be allowing myself that luxury of wanting low effort reward, as I would acknowledge the work required to make my publication circulate more copies. And blogging is essentially a publishing business in the digital age.

Most of the influencer economy is built around this illusion of instant gratification. While it might be true for some lucky virality, generally speaking, success in the influencer world or creator economy is also built around consistently working on your content through the prism of patience, collaboration, and the many other aspects I mentioned before.

This need for instant gratification is starting to affect many other aspects of our lives too. In the early stages of my corporate career, I encountered friends who came into large companies with unrealistic expectations of doing majorly impactful and fulfilling work, right from day one, displaying an impatience when they didn't see that happening, which contributed to a general refusal to learn to play their roles. As I grew to then lead a team of Gen Zers, I only saw this feeling exaggerated in the next generation. We are increasingly wanting to play the lead role, even if our ability is currently that of an extra. That acknowledgment of the time and effort it takes to get from an extra to a lead seems to have been lost on us.

What this also creates is a need to jump jobs more quickly. While there are many factors for this, the prime being pay and benefits, the need for instant gratification shows up in trends. According to Bureau of Labor Statistics data in the US, between 2014 and 2022, we saw a slight decline in the average tenure of the median worker (25–34 years old) from 3 to 2.8 years.[10]

This also affects the way we date today. With the rise of dating apps, all based on admittedly innovative concepts, we are trained to instantly gratify, satisfy, and vilify. It is easier to ghost people than have a real, difficult conversation—something that is preferred by more and more people active in the dating game.

The same choice and dopamine that social media gives us translates to the dating world through the gamification of dating. I was smitten by this too, back in the mid-2010s when these apps were taking over the dating world, spending hours trying to get matches, meeting some very interesting people, but then usually falling back to that empty feeling, swiping again. Eventually, I met my wife in a real-life interaction, through a real-life friend, at an ex-colleague's wedding in India.

Investing and day-trading is another aspect of our lives we see hit by gamification and instant gratification. I see many people in their 20s and 30s gambling away their little life savings on risky investment strategies, trying to find the next bitcoin. The market declines of late 2021 and 2022 hammered home the age-old investment adage of time spent versus timing the market. However, we all know people still trying to make a Gordon Gekko out of themselves.

Care vs. Efficiency

If collective humanity were an animal, we would seem to be a stressed-out, sickly monkey, digging manically in the same hole, trying to find a scrap that it could find engagement in, in exchange for a little hit of dopamine, before frantically moving on to looking for another scrap. With adoption of technology and AI, we are collectively and increasingly losing the ability to value care in our work, the only thing that we can really control. This is something we acknowledged and appreciated for almost all of humanity's existence, and to which we owe much of our progress as the apex predator on Earth. Persistent precision and care took us to the Moon.

One of the formative people in my life, my favorite teacher in school, the late Brother Eric D'Souza, once told me a story that stuck with me—of the monk and the engineer. Every day an engineer on his way to work passes an old monk struggling to get water out of a well with an archaic rope system. The engineer, one day, out of the kindness of his heart, installs a mechanized pulley system to help the old monk get water without much effort. He expects the monk to thank him, but the next day, he sees the monk at it again, with the old rope he was using. Puzzled, the engineer confronts the monk.

The monk explains he'd rather do it his way, as that is the only way he knows to accomplish the task with utmost care. He worried that he didn't need to put in care with the mechanized method, and thus, he wouldn't feel as connected to the task. This is something we can all think about, especially as we seek to be more efficient through AI agents that can do every task we can think of. We may become more efficient, but without the necessary care, we won't feel as connected to our own outputs, something I feel when comparing my work, mostly on slides in the virtual world, to my father's, who builds buildings in the physical world.

Reading history taught me that any significant change in the world takes effort, over a long period of time. The Indian independence movement lasted at least over a century, the French Revolution lasted a decade, the Renaissance lasted two centuries. We seemed to have forgotten that Rome wasn't built in a day.

Even until a few decades ago, humans were okay with sending mail by post and then waiting for a response for weeks. With the invention of email and instant messaging, that has completely changed. While such inventions were meant to free us, they have actually made us miserable prisoners of our own inventions.

A 2019 study by McKinsey found that an average American worker spends about 28 percent of the workday reading and responding to emails. That amounts to about 2.6 hours a day or a staggering 120 messages per day.[11] This was pre-pandemic and with the rise of remote work, this would have only increased. Contrast this to observing my father in the 1990s and even through the 2000s, dedicating a Friday morning to answering company mail. I often thought of him and that image of him serenely, on a day that was overwhelmed and overtaken by my own inundated inbox and pings, writing or typing letters in his home office. Switching off from work, and focusing on it, both seemed easier for previous generations, working with less technology.

In another study, a team of researchers at the University of California, Irvine, sought to study the correlation between email and stress. They monitored the heart rates of 40 employees along with their computer and email usage. The study found that "the longer people spent on emails in a given hour, the higher the stress levels."[12]

They also studied subjects when they were "batch-checking" their inboxes, an often marketed technique to manage email-related stress. They found that for those people who scored high in the trait of neuroticism, batching emails made them feel even more stressed, by the possibility of ignoring important messages. Batch-checking emails, along with turning off email notifications, was helpful for me personally, but initially I had to actively fight those anxious thoughts, reminding myself that "nothing couldn't wait a few hours."

Additionally, a linguistic analysis as a part of the same study concluded that people answered emails with less care when stressed and such emails would be more likely to contain words that expressed anger, thus creating a cycle of unnecessary stress within teams and organizations. Stress that simply satisfies a need for busy-ness, to show others you are on top of things. So, not only are we creating more stress for ourselves and others with the quantity of emails every day, but we are also becoming less empathetic and thoughtful because of it.

In India, we are inundated by instant messaging via Whats-App, an even more intrusive form of technology. Everywhere you go, whether to a grocery store or a restaurant, they ask for your phone number and spam you on WhatsApp. This is because the digital revolution in places like India skipped the desktop, and thus email, and went straight to mobile, and instant messaging. It has a similar impact as email, just even more intrusive and always on.

All the Information but No Power to Process It

In *Stolen Focus*, Johann Hari quotes a study on the amount of information we are subject to today versus a few decades ago.[13] In the 1950s, we had about two newspapers' worth of information thrown at us daily through all media. By 1986, this was at about 40. By 2007, this had increased to 174. Today, thanks mostly to social media and the boom in streaming, we probably get over 2,000 newspapers' worth of information beamed at us every single day of our lives. We are at a stage of complete system overload.

An assumption within capitalism is that more is better. Most technology we surround ourselves with today is focused on "more"—more data, more internet speed, more machines, more memory, more cloud storage, constantly more and more! Thus, as humans we have been getting more and more biased with associating having more of a thing as the most optimal outcome.

We pride ourselves on having more data in our machines and within our own systems, even if most of that data is garbage. We are consumed by the news, not just from around us locally, but also from everywhere in the world. While that endeavor is admirable, it is not sustainable or practical for the human mind, which is a muscle, not an AI chip.

In meditation, no matter what form you practice, there is an emphasis on starting with a few cleansing breaths—both for the mind and the body. This emphasis on clearing your mind temporarily through a focus on breath is an age-old practice. To me, what this intuitively indicates is that our mental systems are designed to work on and actively process very little information. We've convinced ourselves we're multitaskers, but that is a fallacy. Our superpower, as a species, has been to use precise information and knowledge our minds deduce to then focus on executing a task, most optimally in flow states. If you stick with meditation for a few days, you will start feeling a positive, restful emptiness within you that probably leaves you more focused and in flow toward priorities in your life.

Today, we are multidimensionally overloaded with information. Professionally, we interact all day with emails and chats. To "de-stress," we look at Instagram reels and TikTok, which are designed to overload us with bits of random information we don't know what to do with, fueled by an algorithm built to addict your mind to such bite-sized nuggets of information. We are constantly connected with our friends and family through instant messaging and video calls, yet feel disconnected from our immediate physical environments.

Our flow states have been crippled, a superpower stolen from us, by us, and for no real fault of the general us. Our internal systems are simply not meant for such information overload. All systems, man-made or natural, tend to go down under stress or overload. Burnout is a symptom of a system that is trying to shut down, or, in most cases, already has.

In that state, we've been simply too overloaded for too long and the system then craves a hard reset. What makes that harder to accept today, at least for me, is that all these choices were mine alone—to pick up my phone and scroll, to have email notifications turned on to be professional, to be aware of the news from around the world. However, in a way, those choices weren't mine at all.

This need for immediacy and global jobs has meant that people are checking emails and responding to pings, even when not at work. Since I was always working in global roles, with teammates across the world, there would always be an email to check or a ping to answer.

We tried creating rules of engagement across the globe, but they would end up creating even more stress, deciding the best way to handle it was by creating personal boundaries via turning off notifications and other means. We made a conscious effort to make people think about when the email or ping would land on the other side of the world, but there were hundreds of emails flying around from other teams anyway. Also, that feeling like you need an update at 3 a.m., because someone else across the world was in the middle of their workday, was hard to control, and is now a quintessential part of working in global corporations. Giving in to that temptation and then going down another email rabbit hole was commonplace for me and my mentally overwhelmed colleagues.

We are also hyperaware of issues at local, national, and global levels. Yes, there is a lot of crazy stuff in the world and most of the world can do better. However, we are living in the safest period in the history of humanity—by metrics of mortality, life expectancy, education, poverty, and so on. By being hyperaware of the world, we are starting to forget to notice and wander the world around us, wherein the real beauty lies, and the only bits you can truly experience first-hand. But, it isn't your fault.

All this technology was meant to bring about positive outcomes. But for a lot of our mental states, it hasn't. Finding compassion for yourself in that feeling is important. And letting yourself feel that is equally important. Because all of this was marketed to us by powerful forces. The world, and our experience of it, in the last two decades has been built on an experiment, on how much our systems can be overloaded.

With the rise of AI and the elimination of many types of jobs, workplaces might get better in terms of long hours through potentially shorter workweeks. And, in theory, we can empower ourselves by managing the role emails and instant messaging play both in our work and lives. However, we will continue to be inundated with technology trying to monetize our time and create a oneness with it. Additionally, the world's workforce will shift, as it already is, toward an economy built around creative output, playing out on the platforms that are custodians of the internet.

We will have fewer avenues for involuntary attention and flow states unless we actively create them by making space for boredom, nothingness, and rest. This means building a conscious relationship with technology, carving out daily or weekly time for nothingness, having analogue days or weeks, and fighting that urge to get another dopamine hit. If we can do that, collectively as a species, we might end up feeling a little more restful. But tech companies and the way we have evolved to work through instant communication will not make it easy. Eventually, it really will be up to each and every one of us!

CHAPTER 9

A Decline of the Collective

Growing up in India, I was brought up with a people-first mentality. I grew up with about 30 people—parents, a sister, three cousins, two uncles and aunts, grandparents, and three tenant families under one large roof. To a North American, this might seem a bit absurd or nauseating even, and I've had many laughs with my American wife about the eccentricities of that setup. However, in India, the concept of a "joint family" is common and still flourishes, partly through obligation and circumstance, and partly through a sense of belonging.

A vivid memory of my childhood is a picture that hung at a cousin's house. It was taken in the 1970s, of 50-plus people across six families and four generations—kids, parents, grandparents, and great-grandparents filling a large black-and-white frame. The entire family had migrated, after a bloody Indo-Pak partition, from Abbottabad, Pakistan, 2,000 miles east, in

1946–47, to Northeast India, a culture that couldn't be more alien. However, a quarter of a century later, there were new faces, new hope, new lives. My dad, ten or so at the time, his three siblings, my grandfather, grandmother, and great-grandfather were all in that frame.

Another vivid part of my childhood was always having someone to talk to, something I took for granted—cousins, tenants, friends up the street, other people you run into. Across India, tea stalls, something brought to India by the British, facilitated such constant, neighborly exchanges. Those are the places or *nukkads* (street corners) you convene at, organically, out of habit, almost at the same time every day to have a chat about nothing much and everything in the world, over a chai and samosa. It is a bit of *bakchodi* or *bakkar* or *bakaet*, all slang from different parts of India that mean the same thing, just having a fun chat, about everything and nothing, all at once.

There was a sense of simplicity and organic-ness to those relationships, fostered by those spaces, within families and neighborhoods. The sense of duty and collective pride bestowed upon family, along with the trauma of a recent displacement, gave families and neighborhoods a significantly higher importance in social structures. Thus, family and community ties were strong.

The family and community I've just described, though, is diminishing globally. Even my own family and broader community in India have been affected. Due to the lack of opportunity where I am from, only about 10 percent of my generation is still there. As my parents' generation retires, about half are looking to spend their retirement elsewhere, due to the complicated politics of the area.

Modern life, gated communities, and the way we have redesigned society have taken away those organic spaces that facilitated that sense of love, belonging, and connection. Today, whether it is at the church or the office or the store or in the line at the coffee shop, we are all usually looking down at our phones, doing our best to avoid a chat. We actively try to distance ourselves from a sense of belonging, sucked into a world that doesn't physically exist. You don't see that as much with boomers, and as a millennial, I've often wondered how those people just appear a tad happier, despite being so much older and worn out.

We are more and more digitally connected, but socially disconnected. This can also be observed in the lack of political unity, even within similar economic classes. The foundational structures of family and community that were built over thousands of years are being actively questioned and gradually stripped away from our social lives.

Now we tune in to communities that we have found online, while the means through which we found a true sense of belonging offline have dramatically dissipated. It has gotten to a point where you check with a text before even calling your closest friends or family, even when you know they're probably staring at their phone.

Happiness studies have one common finding—the strength and quality of our relationships are the biggest factors in living happier, more fulfilled, and longer lives. It's no surprise that the decline in our sense of belonging to a physical, personal community is a contributing factor to burnout.

Collectivism vs. Individualism

I've now lived over ten years in Europe and the US, married a Midwestern American woman, and worked in a Californian company for 11 years. In my experience, a general difference between ancient Eastern and Western philosophy is the attitude toward the inward versus the outward.

As mentioned earlier, as per my understanding, Western society emphasizes bettering oneself toward a metaphorical conquest of the surrounding world. Eastern society focuses on finding peace and grounding within oneself to then find oneness with the surrounding world, from a place of acceptance over conquest. It presents quite a different mindset and shows up in daily interactions.

Through the COVID pandemic and after, I spent a lot of time with my wife's family in the northern suburbs of Chicago. Family structures, events, dinner routines, and life in general couldn't be more different from where or how I grew up. People tend to self-soothe here. When I was growing up, a problem was hammered out of you, no matter what, to make it everyone's problem. Whether it was then solved is another matter, but the sharing of the problem itself often was helpful in the short term.

One experience that stays with me from visits to where my wife grew up is walking the family dog, Zoey, every day. I usually took her on a two-kilometer walk around the large, sprawling neighborhood. Depending on the weather, I may have passed no more than five people, usually with their dogs, where nobody was in anyone's way.

There are no street corner nukkads, just dog parks with ideal conditions created for dogs to socialize in a controlled environment. The humans try to survive whatever little inter-actions they have with each other around a curated experience for their pets. Outside of the dog parks, on walks, people tend to cross over to the other side of the road when someone else approaches, or hold their dogs to the side, always with a friendly nod but not much conversation beyond that, as if human interactions were bad for their health.

Another experience that is quintessentially American is the drive-through. Having only lived in Manhattan in the US, I was shocked as we drove up to a suburban drive-through ATM terminal back in 2020. That, to this day, has been the most stunned I've been at a truly American invention. In addition to restaurants, suburban America showed me drive-through phar-macies, liquor stores, smoke shops, voting booths, and even vaccination sites.

This drive-through culture in the US is literally the oppo-site of the culture of the nukkad tea stall from back home. Individualism manifests in many other forms in the West, like marriages, for example. In India or most of the East, even parts of Southern and Eastern Europe, weddings are considered a family affair. In the individualistic US and most of Western Europe, they are considered the couple's business with the fam-ily supporting.

With capitalism and Western ideas taking more of a prece-dence in the world, even traditionally collectivist systems are trending more toward individualism. In India, for example, as subsequent generations are earning more, they are offering to pay for houses for their parents, rather than living together. This trend will only accentuate the loneliness pandemic we have perpetuated with technology.

In the US and Canada, there is a concept of a "friendship recession" that has gained popularity in the last few years. It was coined in 2021 after a survey by the Survey Center on American Life, which found that about 15 percent of American men reported having no close friends. This was just 3 percent in 1990.[1] Single men are the worst affected group, as per the study, and in a 2019 research project by R. Garfield and R. Streeter, the prime causes of higher rates of loneliness among millennials was "a decline in lower religious involvement, lower marriage rates and geographical mobility." Moreover, they also found that longer working hours, changing jobs more frequently, and remote work robbed Americans of the most common place where friendships develop—the workplace.[2]

Thus, we live in a world where we have thousands of friends and followers online, one click away. We travel more and more, yet we feel more isolated in our most local surroundings. We have many options to date, but not (m)any we want to commit to.

Needing a Sense of Belonging

One window into why more and more people are burned out might be found in declining marriage and birth rates across the world. Family sizes have reduced and more and more of us are choosing to not marry and have kids.

There are many societal reasons for this decline in birth rates and the family unit in general. As stated earlier, economic models of development have rural to urban migration as a key part of how an economy matures. This means more people are living busy, unaffordable, urban lives today. Cities have gotten extremely expensive, making everything from housing, healthcare, and childcare difficult to afford. Urban migrations also mean you are usually away from your parents and support systems. The village that helped raise kids, that was taken for granted for millennia, simply doesn't exist anymore.

According to OurWorldInData.org, fertility rates around the world have plunged since their peak in the 1970s with only Africa (4.4), Asia (2.2), and Oceania (2.4) remaining above the replacement rate of 2.1.[3] By the end of the century, the world is expected to be in a net negative. Thus, humanity, metaphorically, and numerically, would "peak" around the end of the century.

Along with this change in family dynamics, religion is another element that can bring about an organic sense of community and belonging, but that seems to be diminishing in importance, especially with young people, globally. Growing up, even though neither I nor any of my cousins were religious, we were dragged to the *gurdwara*, or Sikh temple, every Sunday. And we went out of an obligation, but also to hang out with other kids in the community. There was also a little Sikh temple at home maintained by my grandmother and the women of the house.

That brought mini events at home, facilitating more time spent with friends or cousins. While I wasn't religious, standing outside the gurdwara with my friends buying ice cream and chatting is one of my favorite childhood memories. We also got together to do *seva*, or community service—chores in the gurdwara that involved cleaning, cutting, cooking, and serving food. We also had activities like sports days, picnics, and music classes. All that gave us a sense of collective duty and belonging, a role the church plays in the West.

Total fertility rate: births per woman

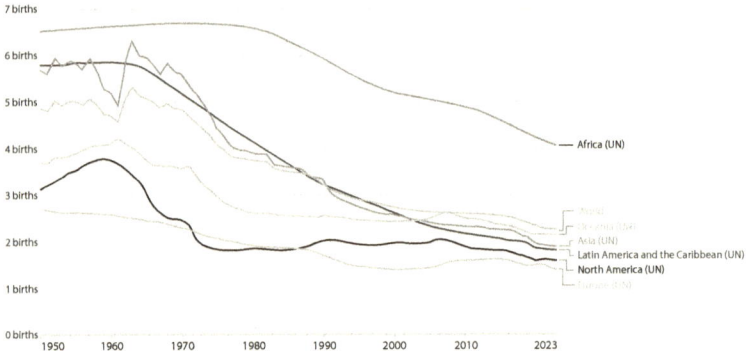

7 births

6 births

5 births

4 births   — Africa (UN)

3 births

2 births   Asia (UN)
                                                                      Latin America and the Caribbean (UN)
                                                                      North America (UN)
1 births

0 births
      1950   1960   1970   1980   1990   2000   2010   2023

(Source: Data from OurWorldInData.org)

Truth is, human beings aren't designed to feel truly fulfilled by making choices for the benefit of just themselves. This is why community, duty, and giving back are part of all religions, in some form, codifying what fulfills humans. This is why most billionaires are into philanthropy. This is why, to achieve self-actualization, as per Maslow's hierarchy of needs theory, humans need love and belonging through friendship, intimacy, and a sense of community. That becomes a bridge toward self-esteem and finally toward self-actualization to help us become what we believe is the best version of us. Family plays a huge role in that path to self-actualization.

The erosion of the family or the collective for the individual has left us stuck in the bottom two layers of Maslow's hierarchy of needs—physiological and safety needs—seeking love and belonging and never truly achieving a sense of self or self-actualization. This leaves us feeling exhausted and confused as we are not being motivated by a larger *why* beyond our own lives. We need a greater cause, a motivator, a driver, a sense of doing it for someone or something. The erosion of those facilitators from our lives has left the world, and probably you, a bit more burned out.

You know what restores faith and connection in humanity like nothing else can? Forming a new connection and going from stranger to friend!

TALK TO
STRANGERS!

BUILD A CONSCIOUS
RELATIONSHIP WITH
TECHNOLOGY

EMBRACE THE
POWER OF
INCREMENTALITY
AND CARE

BE CURIOUS, NOT
JUDGMENTAL
ABOUT YOURSELF

Talk to Strangers!

I've observed a pattern in my life—I'm more prone to feelings of depression when I haven't spoken to a stranger in a while. And as we discussed in chapter 9, our world is rapidly designing itself toward losing this ability to make connections. Most of us are too busy looking down, straining our necks, developing arthritis staring at our phones, avoiding eye contact, and deeming the world around us as the cause of our suffering, rather than a community of shared sufferers—suffering that is being hurled at us through the very phones we stare down at.

Research suggests that talking to strangers can actually help renew us, and even make us smarter and happier! For example, in 2013, psychologists Gillian Sandstrom and Elizabeth Dunn published a result of an experiment in which they had 30 people smile and talk to their barista while another 30 were asked to make their transaction as efficient as possible. The study participants who interacted with the barista felt a deeper sense of belonging and an improved mood versus those who made their transaction extremely efficient.[1]

A natural reason why we avoid talking to strangers is because mustering the courage to talk to a stranger is hard. Additionally, we feel the need to abide by today's societal norm of generally not talking to strangers.

Behavioral scientists Nicholas Epley and Juliana Schroeder at the University of Chicago asked commuters to talk to strangers on mass transit, taxis, and waiting rooms in Chicago, places we actively avoid strangers but places that present us with those opportunities daily. Understandably, most predicted that these interactions would go poorly. They worried about the resentment they would face from strangers and the unpleasantness of the subsequent commute.

However, what they found was that strangers were receptive, curious, and pleasant. "Commuters appeared to think that talking to a stranger posed a meaningful risk of social rejection. As far as we can tell, it posed no risk at all," Epley and Schroeder wrote. It made their commutes pleasant and enjoyable. Epley and Schroeder concluded that this suggests that most of us have a "profound misunderstanding of social interactions" and that "humans may be social animals but not always be social enough for their own well-being."[2]

They've since repeated this study in London and a variety of other countries with a diversity of participants. And, unsurprisingly, results have been consistent.

An office environment has always provided us with an organic space to have chance encounters with strangers, and we can consciously use workspaces as opportunities to connect with strangers.

However, remote and hybrid work has exacerbated the decline in the social importance of the workplace, especially in America. A 2019 paper by Michael Rosenfeld, Reuben Thomas, and Sonia Hausen found that American couples meeting through coworkers reduced from a peak of 20 percent in the 1980s to 1990s to 11 percent in 2019. Today, only 8 percent meet through coworkers. Conversely, 60 percent of American couples now meet online.[3]

This decline of the social aspects of workplaces is an absolute travesty.

One of the things that I missed most while working remote during the pandemic was having these chance encounters with interesting people in a similar context. The decline of in-person meetings reduced the short pleasantries at the beginning to awkward silences behind switched-off cameras. Among the many things that don't make sense about returning to office, access to micro interactions with strangers that refresh you periodically is one that does. Obviously, larger companies like Google afford more access to strangers and spaces that enable these interactions.

Remember our phones and the companies that run them want us to spend our time looking at them endlessly. They monetize your time and engagement on those apps. They often tap into that feeling that we are all familiar with, of the "world probably going to shit." But, if you choose to look up and engage with the world, you find people like you—you feel that the world is a happier, less lonely, more empathetic place, concluding that the world around us isn't that bad after all! That feeling itself is strong enough to help put you on a path to recovery. Why don't you try talking to a stranger today, even if it is just to say hello?

Build a Conscious Relationship with Technology

In chapter 8, we delved into the role technology has played in the decline of our mental fortitude. However, the fact remains that technology is something that is inescapable and critical in today's world. And, as humans, our technology has always given us our edge, our means to advance, our ability to survive—from the rudimentary tools cavemen used to the AI-enabled software I am using to write this book.

While technology has always been with and around us, technology has never been as intrusive as it is today, in every waking minute of our lives. We can thank the invention of the smartphone for that. In my mind, the jury is still out on how successful that invention will prove to be for humanity, especially with how obsessively we've ended up using it. Had the apps that run our smartphones not been trying to addict us and make us infinitely scroll, I'd be more optimistic about it.

In addition, especially if you're under 50, it is important

to recognize that smartphones are a bridge to the next, even more intrusive technology. We are starting to see this through spatial computing and the rise of more immersive tech like AR/VR headsets on a personal level. At a larger scale, technology like face/iris recognition is enabling mass surveillance. As you get older, you will have to fight or tolerate this intrusion even more. Thus, we have never truly needed to build a conscious relationship with technology as much as we need to today.

In terms of most corporate work, we are at a point where we can be always reached through various mediums and always need a screen to execute our duties. Thus, it has become business as usual for work to intrude into personal time. Leaving work at the office is impossible today, as opposed to the 1970s where there was no way to reach you after 6 p.m.

Australia passed a new law in 2024 called the "right to disconnect," which enables employees to ignore work-related contact or attempted contact outside working hours.[1] While these efforts are admirable, they will be limited to developed markets like Australia and aren't very practical. In places like India, where the work culture is intrusive, last minute, and "flexible," corporate workers are almost expected to attend to work on weekends or late at night or their early-morning commutes. I have often seen people on work calls at 1 a.m., despite people being in the same time zone.

Eventually, it will have to be you who will need to define your boundaries. It is well documented that screen time and exposure to blue light is directly proportional to how stressed we feel via the dopamine in our systems. Additionally, intrusive notifications have an adverse effect on stress levels and steal our flow and focus. The good thing is that, especially in the

West, there is an increasing awareness and acceptance of the side effects of such intrusive technology on our mental health.

With this awareness, we have seen the advent of easy tools on our phones like Do Not Disturb or bedtime modes. Use them! These modes usually restrict notifications and eliminate blue light on your screens at set times. They are easy ways to create boundaries that tech companies have created for conscious consumers.

Something that works for me is also turning off email notifications on my phone and having three blocks for emails throughout the day. I also had ping notifications turned off for work chat outside working hours. In places like corporate America, which is obsessed with immediate responses to emails and pings, I had automatic email responders or a status on my ping informing people of when they could expect a response.

Additionally, it is important to carve out and respect that time as sacred. Many tech professionals have such time carved out where they spend time with family or are unavailable for meetings. They also are ensuring that their kids build a healthy relationship with technology, and many tech CEOs do not allow their kids access to phones till they are in their teenage years. This was a topic often discussed at Google.

Eventually, your own boundaries with the invasive technology that surrounds you will determine your peace of mind. It is up to you to protect your own sanity by being conscious about how you use technology, and not letting technology use you. If you don't protect your mental oasis, no one else will.

Embrace the Power of Incrementality and Care

We live in an instantaneous world—of distraction and gratification. One that doesn't allow us to appreciate that life is meant to be a slow, gradual climb up the mountain. We don't want to think about the "eventually." Rather we are made to desire the instantaneous, careless scrambling. However, anything good in life is built carefully, one day at a time. In this world driven by animalistic virality and get rich quick schemes, we are being taught to actively ignore this universal truth.

Imbibing this incrementality, especially when you're stuck in a rut, is easier said than done. I used to constantly beat myself up about not being able to live the life that I should be living—socially, physically, mentally, financially.

As a kid, I was always extremely active and good at multiple sports but was overweight, borderline obese. That continued into my college days, and it got worse as life took over and I found less time to play sports. Growing up where I did, I wasn't imparted a foundational knowledge about nutrition and exercise. Thus, I easily ignored that and carried on with that extra weight.

As I started working at Google Hyderabad, for the first time in my life, I had easy access to nutritious food and a gym with trainers in the office building. On the other hand, we were surrounded by unending free and indulgent food as well. At Google, internal research at the time suggested that the average Googler gained 15 pounds in their first year, known as the "G15." Many of my batchmates fulfilled the "G15."

I, on the other hand, started focusing on getting thinner. The problem lay in my attitude—I focused on getting obsessively thinner, rather than fitter with a good nutritional base. It was based on an obsessive diet where carbs were the enemy, and I allowed myself carbs just once a week. Just like the average New Yorker.

I had transformative results and lost about 40 kilograms (88 pounds), going from 110 kgs (approximately 242 lbs) to about 70 kgs (154 lbs) in 18 months while I was obsessively hitting the gym and playing soccer and cricket. I was obsessed with losing at least 3 kgs (7 lbs) a month, no matter what. I felt amazing, with the newfound attention and having clothes fit me, something I had never really experienced in my life!

However, since my fitness journey was built on a poor and obsessive base, it wasn't sustainable, susceptible to circumstantial derailment. In 2015, three years into my time in Hyderabad, I was looking to move, eventually moving to Dublin, Ireland. As life changed with life getting busier and travel increased, it was hard for me to continue being as obsessive with my gym and diet routine. I started to compensate for that by running ten kilometers thrice a week, to stay thin.

Turns out, I screwed up my knees and triggered an auto-immune condition called Ankylosing Spondylitis due to how much I pushed myself. It was a long and winding diagnosis, as I visited many doctors and umpteen physios in three countries over a year and a half, while moving again internationally to Singapore.

I was also mentally beaten by the lack of a diagnosis and persistent pain. Given my tendency to gain weight, I regained about 30 kgs (66 lbs) over the next three years, leaving me with a despondent, "back to square one" feeling. That despondency then affected other aspects of my life.

While I tried my best to get back on the gym train, the condition had started to affect my back and, even more so, my mental attitude toward physical activity. I wouldn't want to push myself at all and my brain would shut me down as soon as I felt any pain. I started expecting absolutely no soreness after working out, which was unrealistic, even at my fittest. I pined to have that fit body back, while having a deep sense of anger toward my own body—an anger over an inability to push myself, like a few years ago. An anger at having worked so hard and then having let it all go.

That attitude got me to a dark place, one where I completely stopped taking care of my body in any way. I would be achy and sleep-deprived all the time, having convinced myself that there was no point in trying to do anything for my own well-being. What was the point when I couldn't play cricket or soccer like I used to before? What was the point when I couldn't work out six days a week or be as fit as I used to be? I started using

alcohol, food, and video streaming as crutches, ending up a negative, bitter couch potato. All this obviously also influenced the
intensity with which I felt burned out at work.

I was stuck in a cycle of instant gratification and instant
regret. It made me stop liking myself. I had stopped walking
even a few blocks (I love walks!). I had withdrawn from people and things I enjoyed. I was in complete self-destruct mode.
That is when my therapist at the time, sensing a pattern, tried
to get me to think about incremental gain. All this also over-
lapped with COVID and its side effects.

She forced me, with a lot of inertia, to just focus on doing a
bit more than yesterday, however small it was. And approaching the whole situation with a sense of compassion and care
toward myself, and whatever I chose to engage with on the
day. If I just got from my bed to my couch yesterday, I'd then
get myself to go out today. The next day, it was about walking to the street corner and the following day the next block,
and so on. If I couldn't do what I intended, I wouldn't vilify
myself. I would be kind to myself and try again the next day.
I applied the same principle to my diet, work, and the many
other aspects of life that I felt were ruinous. Truth is, nothing is
ever as good or as bad as it seems.

It took a long time and many relapses, but I slowly started
feeling a bit lighter mentally. Over a few months, especially
during the dark days of the first COVID lockdown in New
York City, I picked up yoga. At first it was the deep-stretch,
restorative kind, but over time, I progressed toward yoga
that helped me feel stronger. Yoga helped me slow down and
appreciate the impact of alignment, of the body itself, and the
integration of the body with the mind. That in turn helped

me sleep better, which in turn helped me realize the importance of using sleep as the foundation. I started approaching my wellness with incremental care, rather than looking for a miraculous, instantaneous pill.

In a few more months, with a lot of caution, I also started playing pickup soccer in New York. I was renewed and didn't care about wanting to be 30 kgs (66 lbs) lighter in an instant anymore. I just cared about being able to play 20 minutes a couple of days a week, and accept whatever soreness came with it. That helped me build trust in myself again.

I stopped holding myself to unrealistic standards like only working out if I did it six days a week. I felt more empowered to manage my condition through a combination of yoga, hiking, and sports. Through 2020 and 2021, I traveled across the US twice, visiting about 45 national parks and hiking a lot. It made me connect with nature like I hadn't since I was a little boy in the stunning foothills of the Himalayas in Meghalaya, India.

Today, I'm about 10 kgs (22 lbs) lighter than where I was in my trough. I am stronger, more energetic in life, and mentally curious again. While I can't say that I don't have my demons revisit me from time to time, focusing on careful, incremental gain, or a one-day-at-a-time approach, always brings me back to myself.

So, find whatever helps you feel incremental gain toward something you've been trying to do, but feel exhausted thinking about. The exhaustion happens because of the lack of a realized, incremental gain. Doing something is almost always easier than overthinking it. So, promise yourself one thing you'll incrementally do every day or every week and the rest will take care of itself.

Incrementality and Engaging Exercise

In this bizarre image-driven culture, the gym is marketed as the temple to fulfill our desires for unrealistically sculpted bodies. While the gym can be a temple for some and is extremely important for muscular symmetry, gym culture has become an example of humanity losing perspective around why we need to be fit—to be healthy to live a long, quality life. Our brains have not evolved to desire work for the sake of it.

Think about it. Our ancient relatives *Homo erectus* roamed the planet between about two million to 110,000 years ago, spreading from Africa to all across Eurasia. The species, in stages, then evolved into Neanderthals about 400,000 years ago and *Homo sapiens* around 300,000 years ago.[1] *Homo sapiens* then roamed the planet, hunting and gathering for hundreds of thousands of years before we developed the ability to communicate through language around 50,000 years ago.

We still took another 40,000 years to evolve toward temporary villages using seeds of wild plants for domestic use. We then moved from the Stone Age to the Bronze Age about 6,000 years ago, finally evolving to the Iron Age with national economies and empires about 3,000 years ago!

So, for about 97 percent of our existence and evolution as a species, we were hunter-gatherers foraging the land and walking endlessly to survive. Out in the wild, our priority was accumulating and conserving energy, minimizing work, ensuring energy supplies to run away from the many wild animals around us. We invented tools to hunt and gather more efficiently. All this required long-term incremental care and knowledge, applied to a set of tasks.

While we've convinced ourselves that we aren't animals or

have evolved beyond our animalistic instincts, we are more animalistic than we think. Think about a pride of lions, where a couple of lions may have led the hunt, but everyone eats together. Inviting people to break bread together has formed the basis of human bonds. So, are we that different from a pride of lions?

In terms of physical activity, *Homo sapiens* spent most of their energy walking long distances, occasionally running or climbing and swimming. We surely weren't doing exercise regimens in dedicated spaces.

Our animalistic brains have simply not yet evolved to want unnecessary work, physical or mental, no matter what the burgeoning fitness industry tells you. According to Statista, global health club revenue grew 43 percent in a ten-year period between 2009 and 2019. Despite this, only about 2.4 percent of the world's population in 2019 had a membership. America by far has the highest number of gym goers in the world, with 64.2 million memberships in 2019.[2]

The average gym-going American goes to the gym two days a week with one in five being regular enough to exceed that number. Additionally, according to Statista, about 18 percent of gym members in the US never attend.[3]

Traditional health clubs and fitness studios, which offer things beyond the gym, from spas to cafés to sporting facilities to classes, according to the Fitness Business Association, had about a 71 percent retention rate in 2018, much higher than stand-alone gyms.[4]

Many of us also join the gym not to be fitter every day, but with more cosmetic goals in mind. According to Statista, 44 percent of gym goers said they go to the gym to "be fitter" while 32 percent were going to the gym to "look good." Thirty-one percent joined to "have fun" and 28 percent to "meet new people" or basically to find people to break bread with.[5]

Thus, what is clear is that we might join the gym with certain goals in mind, usually cosmetic, but what keeps us in the gym are things beyond the gym, things that engage us. We are simply not designed to engage with something we do not enjoy. And we should stop beating ourselves up about it. There is a reason tech companies build products to drive engagement. We are just tuned to enjoy the world through feeling engaged. It is why so many of us, or as the stats suggest, one in two, fall by the wayside. If you love the gym, good for you! You're probably more evolved than the average *Homo sapiens*.

Humans were meant to be doing things that engage them and that includes how we choose to stay fit. And unlike what the fitness industry wants you to believe, you don't need a gym or equipment to stay fit and have a long life. Like our ancestors, walking 5,000 to 10,000 steps a day, jogging, and swimming occasionally will keep our muscles in good shape. Finally, a combination of body and mind, something codified in the ancient Indian practice of yoga, will ensure you are in sync with yourself, something we mostly ignore in organized, mass modern fitness.

A more sustainable strategy, rather than joining a new gym in January (12 percent of all gym memberships begin in January)[6] and quitting by March, is to choose a few activities that you enjoy, and do them regularly and incrementally. If you enjoy the activity, and feel a sense of connection, it is likely that you will stick by it, and find care while engaging with it. Stop being so obsessed with having a six-pack and focus on what engages both your body and mind and makes you feel well, rather than lean.

For me, I have found a happy balance of hiking, golf, soccer, and badminton combined with yoga and band workouts. I can't label myself fit by any stretch, and could do much better, but a balance between nutrition and activity has me feeling better than I have ever felt. And, as with most things mental, the brain is just looking for a signal from the body. So, find what makes your body give your brain that signal, and just focus on enjoying that activity a couple of days a week, no matter what Instagram tells you. And incorporate the gym as a healthy enabler for the activities you enjoy. Finding connection with physicality will also help lighten your mental load, hopefully fizzling your burnout away.

Be Curious, Not Judgmental about Yourself

We explored in chapter 7 that people differ in their emotional responses to events, based on their own unique operating systems and personalities. We also know that life is 1 percent action, 99 percent reaction. So, it is in your best interest to try to understand your responses to life's happenings. And then, use that knowledge to optimize future emotional responses. If you repeatedly feel a pattern of negative behaviors that you curse yourself about, like binge eating or streaming, for example, approaching that pattern with curiosity rather than judgment is a better strategy.

When you're constantly trying to change how you feel, rather than just feeling what you feel, you fall into the trying trap, a mental mode where you're constantly judging negative feelings, and then judging yourself for not being able to change your state of mind. It creates a negative reinforcement cycle. When you lead with curiosity instead, you are in a mental mode defined by awareness and an acceptance of your emotions and feelings. Judgment creates stress and resistance at a neurological level. Curiosity creates an empowering awareness of your own experience.

Think about a repeated pattern you don't like much. It could be overthinking and over-preparing for meetings, for example. Think about a meeting that you perceived as extremely stressful, either before, during, or after it. Now think about a colleague, or your boss, involved in the same project or meeting and their emotional response. Did they seem less or more stressed out about it? Were they calmer and more composed than you in thought and action? To give you a sports analogy, think about how a rookie's emotional response to a nail-biting game is different from a veteran's.

While we know that people react differently to the same event, a concept emerging in psychology is the judgment people associate with what they feel. People simply judge negative emotions more than positive ones. Think about it. Have you ever questioned joy?

In a 2023 study published in the journal *Emotion,* by the American Psychological Association, researchers found that people who habitually judge negative emotions such as stress, sadness, fear, or anger as bad have more depression and anxiety and feel less fulfilled with their lives than people who perceive their negative emotions in a positive or neutral manner.[1]

We know this is intuitively true as we are usually nonjudgmental about positive emotions. It is the natural thing to do. You let yourself feel happiness, joy, pride, and simply bask in them. You don't resist in any way. According to Iris Mauss, a social psychologist at UC Berkeley and a coauthor of the study, "Many of us have this implicit belief that emotions themselves are bad. Emotions don't do harmful things. It is actually the judgement that causes, ultimately, the suffering."[2]

When we perceive our emotions through a judgmental lens, we compound the negativity of the moment, making us feel even worse. It is likely to increase the weight of negative feelings and the time we spend suffering.

The same is true for our perception and experience of pain too. In a small clinical trial, researchers asked people to put one of their hands in a bucket of ice and either to accept the feelings of pain or suppress them. Those who tried to suppress their pain reported more pain and vice versa.[3]

Essentially, what you resist persists. And this persistence of negative emotions makes regular situations more stressful for such individuals.

As part of the study mentioned earlier, Dr. Mauss and her team asked individuals to either accept their emotions or judge them as bad. Then they asked subjects to give a three-minute speech about their qualifications for a job—a task known to induce stress. Participants who said they didn't usually accept their emotions reported experiencing more negative feelings while giving their speech—an indication of lower self-worth.[4]

By accepting negative emotions as an inevitable part of the human experience, we take away the control we allow these emotions over ourselves. One of my favorite meditation practices revolves around letting yourself feel whatever you're feeling. If you'd like, try it now.

Find a comfortable position, either seated or lying down. I prefer lying down with a pillow under my knees, but it is up to you. Take a few deep breaths to settle in. If it helps, turn on ambient music to help you focus. Once you feel settled in your breath and space, force yourself to think about an extremely negative experience in the past. Force yourself to feel those sights, sounds, and conversations associated with that experience. Just try to breathe evenly as you are doing this. If it helps, breathe in and out in counts of four, pausing for four counts in between.

You might notice that as you let yourself relive that negative experience, you feel an awareness in some part of your body. For me, it is usually my lower back or my thighs. Where I feel it also changes based on what I focus on. It is essentially where the body kept score. And as you keep letting yourself feel these negative emotions and bring awareness to the parts of your body that feel it, you might notice a mild or even radical dissipation of the uneasiness you feel in your body. Merely the awareness and acceptance of that pain reduces it. It is revolutionary!

Now, think about the opposite. Think about an extremely positive experience in the past. Think about the sights, sounds, and conversations associated with that experience. Now bring your awareness to where you feel it in your body. For me, I usually feel this in my chest and neck. Not surprisingly, some of the postural challenges I have are in relation to my chest and neck and doing this instantly helps me feel those parts in alignment again.

Doing this practice regularly helps me build neutrality and a comfortable relationship with my emotions—not too high, not too low. It also helps me separate my behavior and my emotions, and not let what I feel on the day drive my behavior. That helps build consistency and eventually brings a steely emotional resilience.

We live in a world that I believe promotes toxic positivity, even at times when a situation should be felt as negative. We force ourselves to avoid negativity and embrace positivity, at all costs, even when we know most of life is ordinary, and painful. This was especially true in the intensely Californian atmosphere of Google. If this positivity is based in a vehement avoidance of any negativity, it is problematic and often delusional, leading you down a path of anxious avoidance. It is merely postponement, a Band-Aid on a cut that requires stitches.

There is power in letting yourself truly accept and feel the negativity within you, without judgment or resistance. The first step in fixing a problem is acknowledging it exists. Similarly, the first step in feeling less burned out is acknowledging that you are burned out and letting yourself sit with that feeling. Become aware of it—feel it in your bones, make it your own, and, if it helps, let yourself even break down. It might be uncomfortable today, but I promise you, it will be less uncomfortable tomorrow. And eventually, by slowly stripping away the power you gave your own burnout, you likely won't feel as burned out anymore.

You Can't Ride a Bike without Riding a Bike

In the current design of society, our education, corporate structures, and economic incentives push us down a path of building financially sustainable careers. We aren't incentivized or taught to build emotionally sustainable careers or lives. Thus, we naturally expect emotional rewards to accompany financial milestones. When that doesn't happen, we feel emotionally unstable, confused, and burned out.

To alleviate those feelings of burnout, you may decide taking a long vacation or sabbatical could help you feel better. And it might, for a while, or even a long time, maybe. However, your burnout is likely to reemerge if you lack a deeper awareness of what drove you to that exhausted state, the *why* behind it—the role played by systems and structures you live and work within. Building that awareness can put you back on a path of emotional sustainability.

With that awareness, you may also recognize that you have an ever-ongoing emotional tug-of-war inside between the expected path you're on and an alternate, romanticized path. This alternate path can be as simple as another job function within the same company or industry or something more seismic, like a career switch. Perhaps you've imagined yourself being an actor, a sports star, a comedian, a writer, a founder, a musician, or whatever else engaged you through your youth, accompanied by a strong feeling that you could have made it on that path.

The pining for another path is natural. Today's economic environment offers potentially infinite paths to the individual. And we are more aware than ever of those alternate paths through social media and the internet. I follow everyone from carpenters to chocolatiers to fashion designers to drone exterminators on social media. As a corporate worker, you're in an environment where you are hyperaware of these alternate paths, while feeling locked into experiencing a single path. The promise of infinite possibility, with the reality of needing to walk a particular path, is emotionally challenging to navigate. What burns you out, in addition to the fear of losing the stability you have worked so hard to achieve, is the fear of not mustering the strength to take a shot and have a new experience.

We are designed to learn and experience life in two ways—form and feel. Form refers to all the technical, formulaic aspects related to a task or skill, for example the immense technicality of a golf swing. Feel refers to how the body and mind physically register experiencing a task or skill. In the golf swing example, this could be how a particular type of shot feels in your hands versus another type of shot.

While there is no doubt that you need both to master a skill, often, form overwhelms and complicates the purity of feel. This is often why athletes find it hard to answer what was going through their minds while executing an athletic maneuver. That maneuver is stored in their subconscious, after repeatedly experiencing its feel over the years. To the point that it is hard for them to condense it into form.

As humans, we are biased toward predictable instructions while learning, through structured trainings, and other ways in which we have condensed complex mathematical and scientific concepts into easy to digest formulae. Thus, we desire and prioritize formulaic instructions when faced with a new, uncertain task. This is the bias our technically bent, methodical education system has created in us.

The traditional, pyramidical corporate structure is also designed to deliver a formulaic path, biasing our minds when thinking about our careers. However, it is the feel of something, storing it in our subconscious via experience, that helps our minds execute with clarity and confidence.

Natural learning only happens via experience, through feel. Think back to when you learned how to ride a bike, or to swim. You may have stumbled in fear, falling off your bike, scraping your elbows and knees. But you got back up on it, and in a magical moment, your body felt that sweet sense of balance. The same process is true for that moment you felt like you could float on water using your breath. And just like that, as your body experienced a split second of feel, you knew how to ride a bike or to stay afloat, and that feel was forever stamped into your subconscious.

You can't ride a bike without riding a bike! You must condense all the complexity of balancing those two wheels into a feel that is as natural as walking. Remember, your brain repeated this natural learning process when you learned to crawl, walk, run, or perform any motion you take for granted today. There is no substitute for natural, experiential learning. The labor market literally tells us that, by naturally setting higher wages for people with longer years of experience. While we constantly seek form, to help make the path ahead seem more certain, the magic happens when we feel.

In corporate work, you usually have, and desire, a formulaic path to walk ahead, up to a certain point in your career. When the formulaic path becomes unclear or punishing, the uncertainty or the lack of form for the path ahead naturally brings anxiety about what's next, while you feel the continuous pressure of systemic progress—promotions, position, status, and so on. Additionally, bigger paychecks and the corporate ladder disincentivize "finding a feel" for something else by having a different experience. Moreover, the awareness of both form and feel go missing from your pining for that alternate existence. The only way out of this malaise is by finding a rest stop or an off-ramp from the burnout highway to experience something new, enabling a fresh wave of natural learning.

What we often tend to ignore, especially in trancelike states of exhaustion, is that mustering the strength to find a feel for something else doesn't always have to be an all-or-nothing play. There are incremental baby steps you can take to find out whether that alternate existence is even feasible. You may think you could be a stand-up comic, but unless you go to an open mic, how will you know? And how will you know if you even enjoy the process of comedy?

If you aren't ready to take the off-ramp, and head to a completely different highway, switch lanes for a bit to find a feel. The AI, gig, and creator economy has made this so much easier. As a corporate worker, you have an incentive to diversifying your skill sets and having backup paths. The AI-driven economy we find ourselves in is demanding flexible, unconventional careers that focus on many skills and a personal brand. Unconventional careers are the ones that will be able to adapt to a rapidly evolving economic context.

While AI has taken away jobs, it is creating opportunities for the individual economy to flourish. You can now be a filmmaker without needing to shoot, or prototype an app from an idea in a matter of hours without knowing any code. While all this might feel overwhelming, the only way to look at it is that these are tools to help you grow your personal economy.

The marriage of the internet with AI has made labor markets global in nature and the future is the creator and the gig economy. Companies are looking to do things cheaper and quicker and the steady rise in unemployment rates for 22–27-year-olds with a college degree in the US only solidifies this trend. In September 2024, 5.7 percent of workers with a bachelor's degree or higher were unemployed, a higher level only seen after the 2008 crisis and the COVID pandemic.[1]

Thus, investing in your own personal economy and skills, especially as a mid-senior-level employee, is a way to future-proof yourself. My subsistence is driven by having five income streams within five years, something that helps me hedge against the uncertainties of the AI economy and putting too much pressure on any one of my ventures. This also enables me to live a life of variety, one of my core values, enriching myself constantly through natural, experiential learning.

Find some discipline and set aside a couple of hours every week, or more if you'd like, to learn a skill you've procrastinated on, engage with a hobby in an organized manner, or set up a side hustle that you think could become an alternate path. If you're trying to change roles or companies, dedicate time and discipline to relevant upskilling and finding a way to explore it.

At Google, I loved the concept of the 20 percent project, where you could find cross-functional projects to work on for a fifth of your time. Some of my most fulfilling work at Google was through 20 percent projects. To the dismay of some of my bosses, there were times I had five 20 percent projects, in addition to my core job.

By engaging with that alternate path more consciously, you can determine whether a new path is even feasible for the life and goals you have set for yourself. If you can't think of anything you want to do, learn the basics of investing. Investing is the easiest way of creating wealth, and solving for financial independence is another practical way of finding a future off-ramp from the burnout highway. I would argue you should do whatever you choose to do, in addition to learning about investing, and start, as soon or as small as you can.

Couple your investing with clear financial goals based on an audit of your current financial situation, values, and desired path ahead. An amazing site to do that is PortfolioVisualizer.com or just start by educating yourself gently via YouTube.

Just taking small, incremental steps toward that alternate existence and finding a feel for it will empower you, either with the strength to continue on a new path or with the knowledge that you might not be built for it. And if, at the end of it, you feel like the answer is that you are best suited to the path you're on, that's great! Now, you have clarity instead of existential dread. And, you also have perspective on what role your work plays in your life. Additionally, you've enriched yourself with natural learning via a new experience.

Eventually, empowering yourself by feeling out an alternate path or having the knowledge that the alternate path is not for you is what will rid you of that fear. Take it from someone who spent two years publishing this book and is trying to make it as a writer, life coach, corporate consultant, investor, and entrepreneur. I can't say I am completely rid of fear as this path has brought its own struggles, but I can say that that feeling of fear is more and more fleeting. It is a friendlier fear, one that feels more choiceful than the fears of my past.

And for now, at this moment in my life, that state of being is enough for me, in addition to my investments that support my subsistence, of course. If you don't have such a cushion, or the desire to adjust your life to a different financial reality, you have no option but to engage with your alternative existence, in a more conservative manner, through a side hustle or a 20 percent project of sorts. And that is completely feasible too. You just have to choose to be okay with the choice you made for yourself.

As you've learned, the fear-led mindset that drives burn-out originates in a frustrated stuck-ness you feel with your own choices. Choices that were based in the fear that you chose and the fear that drove subsequent choices.

Rather than the fear of never being able to go back to a stable job if I fail in building this life that increasingly makes sense just to me, I have, with a lot of effort, chosen to focus on what helps me build a life that supports my own emotional sustainability. Like my golf swing, I now let the feel of my experiences lead me to the form, building a deep connection with the tasks or skills I'm engaging with. You can also choose to approach your daily work in the same way, making it more mindful and fulfilling.

I also am not as tied to time-bound outcomes, monetary or otherwise, something the formulaic corporate path always laid out in front of me. I have chosen to move forward with a con-fidence that if I am ready to go back to the corporate world, an opportunity will present itself because I will be stronger for this experience. I'll have a better perspective on what role a job plays in my life, something that was missing through a large part of my corporate career, when I didn't have a feel for other experiences. I also believe I'll be a better corporate worker, for everyone involved.

Take a breath and make a plan, to take a chance on your-self, with a commitment to what engages you, is aligned with your values and, most importantly, caters to your own emo-tional needs. Don't think of it as something that will change your life. Treat the process as exploratory, without putting too much pressure on the outcome you think you desire. The only one that can rid you of that stifling fear is you, by building a life that might only make sense to you.

Whatever life you build, building it with a conscious understanding and awareness of the *why* behind your experience will help you get to the root causes of your own exhaustion and avoid it in the future. That self-discovering journey will inevitably take you down a path of uncovering many aspects of your evolving context that formed the basis of your life path. Without an understanding of those roots, it is inevitable that your experience with burnout will be cyclically repeated, when there is a similar set of circumstances that pop up in your life again—a toxic boss, poor corporate structure, a misalignment of your values and work.

By understanding the interactions of the elements that govern our collective experiences, we are empowered with an awareness of why we are feeling the way we do. And with that empowerment, we can take steps toward healing, slowly moving from a narrative of blame to a narrative of acceptance, one that lifts us toward gratitude with a readjustment of our expectations.

And what is life if not a constant evaluation of expectation versus reality? In a world driven by lofty expectations, usually set through marketing propaganda, take a step back and understand that those expectations were set for you by a narrative that might not have been based in your own reality. And, once you have a better understanding of that reality, you can optimize the equation to what matters to you. It is important to appreciate your journey as your own, defined by systems that affect us all. I hope this book has helped you rethink your own journey with burnout with a bit more incrementality, care, curiosity, and compassion. I truly wish you the best of luck.

ACKNOWLEDGMENTS

Writing a book itself is a solitary act, but it is a journey no one makes alone. This book and my perspective have been enabled by a global community of friends, family, colleagues, and well-wishers who have contributed, directly and indirectly, to this book. The insights in this book are based on years of observation, experience, and connection, with some amazing people. I consider myself extremely fortunate to have been able to foster these connections without whom this book would not have been possible.

Firstly, I would like to thank the entire team at Greenleaf Book Group. Being my first book, navigating a whole new process and industry was overwhelming. However, the team at Greenleaf, across the entire publishing process, have been a comforting presence. I would particularly like to thank Judy Marchman, the developmental editor on this book. Without her contribution, the book would be a very different product. I am also extremely thankful to the graphic design team at Chashmaagraph, who helped bring the book to life visually.

To all the friends and family who were early readers and

sounding boards, I cannot express how much your inputs framed the development of the book. I would particularly like to thank Shouvik Sachdeva, Saurabh Dangwal, and Karan Chilana for their support and insight throughout the process.

To all my colleagues, past and present, this book is framed by our paths crossing. Some of my closest friends are people I met at work, and I can't imagine life without them. You've given me endless emotional support and been my guinea pigs for various surveys and efforts like the *Wide World View* podcast. Truly, thank you!

I also want to mention my ex-bosses, who led with such enabling psychological safety: Piedad Rodriguez, Pedro Pina, Ishan Chatterjee, David Saez, Raja Dutta, Kim Larson, amongst others. It is the cultures they set on various teams that helped me nurture many of the insights I bring forth in the book.

To my wife, Melissa, I want to thank you for your unquestioning and endless support through my idiosyncratic ways—in addition to being my earliest reader, critic, and counselor for everything through this long project. To my parents, thank you for fostering the opportunities that led me on this path. In a way, everything I've learned comes through you. To my American family in Illinois, thank you for your love and support through difficult times.

And finally, to you, whoever is reading this. I thank you for giving me the opportunity to help you forge your path ahead, hopefully with new insight and awareness of the path that led you here.

To anyone and everyone who realizes the power of perspective, this book belongs to all of you. Thank you for making it possible.

NOTES

Introduction

1. World Health Organization, "Burn-Out an 'Occupational Phenomenon': International Classification of Diseases," May 28, 2019, https://www.who.int/news/item/28-05-2019-burn-out-an-occupational-phenomenon-international-classification-of-diseases.

2. US Bureau of Labor Statistics, "American Time Use Survey—2024 Results," June 26, 2025, https://www.bls.gov/news.release/pdf/atus.pdf; US Bureau of Labor Statistics, "Average Hours Employed People Spent Working on Days Worked by Day of Week," https://www.bls.gov/charts/american-time-use/emp-by-ftpt-job-edu-h.htm. (Based on average hours worked per week.)

3. Jack Flynn, "20+ Alarming Burnout Statistics [2023]," Zippia, March 30, 2023, https://www.zippia.com/advice/burnout-statistics/.

4. Future Forum, "Future Forum Pulse," February 2023, https://futureforum.com/research/future-forum-pulse-winter-2022-2023-snapshot/.

5. Google Trends, "Occupational Burnout," https://trends.google.com/trends/explore?date=today%205-y&q=%2Fm%2F01v4y_&hl=en-GB.

6. US Bureau of Labor Statistics, "Employment—Population Ratio," https://www.bls.gov/charts/employment-situation/employment-population-ratio.htm.

Chapter 1

1. Wikipedia, s.v. "Euronext Amsterdam," last modified March 24, 2025, https://en.wikipedia.org/wiki/Euronext_Amsterdam.

2. Olga Robert, "10 Oldest Stock Exchanges in the World," Good Returns, June 11, 2019, https://www.goodreturns.in/classroom/2019/06/10-oldest-stock-exchanges-in-the-world-964465.html.

3. Adam Smith, *The Wealth of Nations*, ed. Ludwig von Mises (Martino, 2015).

4. Wikipedia, s.v. "Dutch East India Company."

5. Wikipedia, s.v. "Dutch East India Company," last modified July 14, 2025, https://en.wikipedia.org/wiki/Dutch_East_India_Company#:~:text=Statistically%2C%20the%20VOC%20eclipsed%20all,goods%20carried%20by%20the%20VOC.

6. Wikipedia, s.v. "History of Slavery," last modified July 12, 2025, https://en.wikipedia.org/wiki/History_of_slavery.

7. Daron Acemoglu, Simon Johnson, and James Robinson, "The Colonial Origins of Comparative Development: An Empirical Investigation," *American Economic Review* 91, no. 5 (December 2001): 1369–1401, doi: 10.1257/aer.91.5.1369.

8. Alfred W. Crosby, *Ecological Imperialism: The Biological Expansion of Europe, 900-1900,* 2nd ed. (Cambridge University Press, 2004).

9. *Encyclopedia Britannica,* s.v. "British Railways," https://www.britannica.com/money/British-Railways#ref114145.

10. Wikipedia, s.v. "Indian Railways," last modified July 5, 2025, https://en.wikipedia.org/wiki/Indian_Railways.

11. Elias Beck, "Working Conditions in the Industrial Revolution," History Crunch, March 25, 2022, historycrunch.com/working-conditions-in-the-industrial-revolution.html#/.

12. Wikipedia, s.v. "Trade Union," last modified July 19, 2025, https://en.wikipedia.org/wiki/Trade_union.

13. *Encyclopedia Britannica,* s.v. "Combination Acts," accessed July 3, 2025, https://www.britannica.com/money/organized-labor/The-developing-world.

14. Wikipedia, s.v. "Trade Union."

15. Wikipedia, s.v. "Trade Union."

16. United Nations Department of Economic and Social Affairs Population Division, "World Population Prospects Data," https://population .un.org/wpp/.

17. Andrew Bary, "Google Parent Alphabet Has Had a Rough Year. Investors Should Buy Up Shares," *Barron's*, December 30, 2022, https:// www.barrons.com/articles/buy-alphabet-stock-google-51672341993.

18. United States Security and Exchange Commission, *Annual Report Pursuant to Section 13 or 15(D) of the Securities Exchange Act of 1934 for the Fiscal Year Ended December 31, 2024: Alphabet Inc.* (United States Security and Exchange Commission), p. 35, https://abc.xyz/assets /77/51/9841ad5c4fbe85b4440c47a4df8d/goog-10-k-2024.pdf.

19. Layoffs.fyi, "Layoffs Tracker."

20. Stefon Walters, "The Nasdaq Is Up 20% Halfway Through 2024. Here's What History Says Could Happen in the Second Half," The Motley Fool, July 3, 2024, https://www.fool.com/investing/2024/07/03/ the-nasdaq-is-up-20-halfway-through-2024-heres/.

Chapter 2

1. Worldometer, "India Population (Live)," https://www.worldometers .info/world-population/india-population/.

2. Aggam Walia, "42.3% of Graduates Under 25 Unemployed, Finds Latest State of Working India Report," *Indian Express,* September 21, 2023, https://indianexpress.com/article/business/42-3-of -graduates-under-25-unemployed-finds-latest-state-of-working-india -report-8949124/.

3. Ministry of External Affairs, India, "Population of Overseas Indians," https://www.mea.gov.in/images/attach/nris-and-pios_1.pdf.

4. "India Received $83 Billion in Remittances in 2020: World Bank Report," *Business Standard,* May 13, 2021, https://www.business -standard.com/article/economy-policy/india-received-usd83-billion-in -remittances-in-2020-world-bank-report-121051300108_1.html.

5. Atlas of Humanity, "Indians in the World," https://www
    .atlasofhumanity.com/indians.

6. Wikipedia, s.v., "Kalinga (Region)," last modified July 8, 2025, https://
    en.wikipedia.org/wiki/Kalinga_(region).

7. Wikipedia, s.v. "Indian Indenture System," last modified May 25,
    2025, https://en.wikipedia.org/wiki/Indian_indenture_system.

8. Wikipedia, s.v. "Indian Indenture System."

9. Vazira Fazila-Yacoobali Zamindar, "India–Pakistan Partition 1947
    and Forced Migration," in *Encyclopedia of Global Human Migration*
    (John Wiley & Sons, 2013), https://doi.org/10.1002/9781444351071.
    wbeghm285.

10. Wikipedia, s.v. "British Indians," last modified June 13, 2025, https://
    en.wikipedia.org/wiki/British_Indians.

11. Ruchi Singh, "Origin of World's Largest Migrant Population, India
    Seeks to Leverage Immigration," Migration Policy Institute, March 9,
    2022, https://www.migrationpolicy.org/article/india-migration
    -country-profile.

12. John Calabrese, "India-Gulf Migration: A Testing Time," Middle East
    Institute, April 14, 2020, https://www.mei.edu/publications/india-gulf
    -migration-testing-time.

13. Ankita Sanyal, "Bilateral Issues," *India Speaks,* no. 110 (September
    2018), http://www.mei.org.in/is110; "Question No.1780 Indians
    Returning from Gulf Countries," Ministry of External Affairs:
    Media Center, August 2, 2018, https://mea.gov.in/rajya-sabha
    .htm?dtl/30220/QUESTION_NO1780_INDIANS_RETURNING_
    FROM_GULF_COUNTRIES.

14. Ministry of Statistics & Programme Implementation, "Household
    Social Consumption: Education in India as Part of the 75th Round of
    National Sample Survey—from July 2017 to June 2018," National
    Statistical Office, https://cprindia.org/wp-content/uploads/2023/10/
    NSS-75th-Round-Key-Indicators-of-Household-Social-Consumption
    -on-Education-in-India-July-2017-June-2018-2019.pdf; "Literacy Day:
    At 96.2%, Kerala Tops Literacy Rate Chart Andhra Pradesh Worst
    Performer at 66.4%," *Indian Express,* September 8, 2020, https://
    indianexpress.com/article/education/literacy-day-at-96-2-pc-kerala
    -tops-literacy-rate-chart-andhra-pradesh-worst-performer-at-66-4
    -pc-6587548/.

15. Singh, "Origin of World's Largest Migrant Population."

16. "Indian Nationals Received over 72% of All H-1B Visas Issued from Oct 2022–Sept 2023," *Economic Times,* June 27, 2025, https://economictimes.indiatimes.com/nri/work/indian-nationals-received-over-72-pc-of-all-h1b-visas-issued-from-oct-2022-sept-2023-govt/articleshow/117997429.cms?from=mdr.

17. International Labor Organization, "ILOSTAT Data Explorer," https://rshiny.ilo.org/dataexplorer1/?lang=en&id=SDG_0851_SEX_OCU_NB_A.

18. World Bank Group, "Gini Index," https://data.worldbank.org/indicator/SI.POV.GINI.

19. "India to Become $10-trillion Economy by 2035: CEBR," *Economic Times,* December 26, 2022, https://economictimes.indiatimes.com/news/economy/policy/india-to-become-10-trillion-economy-by-2035-cebr/articleshow/96526283.cms; Statista, "Forecast of the Gross Domestic Product of the United States from Fiscal Year 2024 to Fiscal Year 2034," https://www.statista.com/statistics/216985/forecast-of-us-gross-domestic-product/.

Chapter 3

1. Wikipedia, s.v. "University of al-Qarawiyyin," last updated June 18, 2025, https://en.wikipedia.org/wiki/University_of_al-Qarawiyyin.

2. Nalanda University, "History and Revival," https://nalandauniv.edu.in/about-nalanda/history-and-revival/.

3. Open Access, "University of Paris," https://www.omicsonline.org/universities/University_of_Paris/.

4. Perley G. Nutting, "The Principles of Education," *The Scientific Monthly* 7, no. 5 (November 1918): 448–56, https://www.jstor.org/stable/7005.

5. Nutting, "Principles of Education."

6. Wikipedia, s.v. "General Education Board," last modified May 10, 2025, https://en.wikipedia.org/wiki/General_Education_Board.

7. Louise E. Fleming and Rita S. Saslaw, "Rockefeller and General Education Board Influences on Vocationalism in Education, 1880–1925" (paper presented at Midwestern Educational Research

Association, October 1992), https://files.eric.ed.gov/fulltext/ED349475.pdf.

8. Fleming and Saslaw, "Rockefeller and General Education Board."

9. National Testing Agency, "NTA Declares the Final NTA Scores for Joint Entrance Examination (Main)—2023 for Paper 1," April 29, 2023, https://nta.ac.in/Download/Notice/Notice_20230502163550.pdf.

10. National Center for Education Statistics, "Digest for Education Statistics," https://nces.ed.gov/programs/digest/d23/tables/dt23_330.10.asp.

11. Federal Reserve Bank of St. Louis, "Real Median Household Income in the United States," https://fred.stlouisfed.org/series/MEHOINUSA672N.

12. Alicia Hahn, "Student Loan Debt Statistics: Average Student Loan Debt," *Forbes,* April 18, 2024 https://www.forbes.com/advisor/student-loans/average-student-loan-debt-statistics/#:~:text=The%20federal%20student%20loan%20portfolio,breaks%20down%20by%20loan%20type.

13. Jeffrey M. Jones, "More in U.S. Retiring, or Planning to Retire, Later," Gallup, July 22, 2022, https://news.gallup.com/poll/394943/retiring-planning-retire-later.aspx.

14. "2024 MassMutual Retirement Happiness Study," MassMutual and PSB Insights survey, January 26 to February 5, 2024, https://www.massmutual.com/global/media/shared/doc/2024_massmutual_retirement_happiness_study.pdf.

15. Jones, "More in U.S. Retiring."

16. National Association of Colleges and Employers, *Salary Survey* (NACE, 2022), https://careers.unc.edu/wp-content/uploads/2022/02/NACE-Salary-Survey_Winter-2022.pdf.

17. Federal Reserve Bank of St. Louis, "Median Sales Price of Houses Sold for the United States," https://fred.stlouisfed.org/series/MSPUS.

18. "Educated but Unemployed, a Rising Reality for US College Grads," Oxford Economics, May 27, 2025, https://www.oxfordeconomics.com/resource/educated-but-unemployed-a-rising-reality-for-us-college-grads/#:~:text=Structural%20shifts%20in%20tech%20hiring,t%20shifting%20their%20job%20searches; Reshma Kapadia, "It's a

Bleak Job Market for New College Grads. These Are the Unluckiest,"
Barron's, June 9, 2025, https://www.barrons.com/articles/job-market
-new-college-grads-b31b2424; Giselle Thomas, "A Study Finds that
Recent College Grads Are Struggling to Get Hired," WFMY News 2,
June 5, 2025, https://www.wfmynews2.com/article/money/study-finds
-recent-college-grads-are-struggling-hired-oxford-economics-job/83
-45643593-c254-4740-8e57-57158a2f7921.

19. Sleep Junkie, "The Cities with the Highest Burnout," https://www
.sleepjunkie.com/cities-with-highest-burnout/.

Chapter 4

1. "Workplace Burnout Survey—Burnout Without Borders,"
HealthManagement, June 23, 2024, https://healthmanagement.org/c/
hospital/Post/workplace-burnout-survey-burnout-without-borders;
Aleksandar Dimovski, "28+ Unbiased Millennials in the Workplace
Statistics," GoRemotely, March 31, 2023.

2. Lucas Chancel, Thomas Piketty, Emmanuel Saez, and Gabriel
Zucman, *World Inequality Report, 2022* (World Inequality Lab,
2021), https://wir2022.wid.world/www-site/uploads/2021/12/
WorldInequalityReport2022_Full_Report.pdf.

3. US Inflation Calculator, "Current US Inflation Rates: 2000–2025,"
https://www.usinflationcalculator.com/inflation/current-inflation-rates/.

4. Google Finance, "S&P 500," https://www.google.com/finance/quote/.
INX:INDEXSP?window=5Y (accessed July 28, 2025).

5. Fredric Jameson, *Postmodernism, or, the Cultural Logic of Late
Capitalism* (Duke University Press, 1992).

6. Jameson, *Postmodernism.*

7. Companies Market Cap, "Largest Companies by Marketcap," https://
companiesmarketcap.com.

8. *Oil and Gas Global Market Report 2024* (Business Research
Company, 2024), https://www.thebusinessresearchcompany.com/
report/oil-and-gas-global-market-report.

9. "Indian Inspectors Order Recall of Maggi Noodles, Say Found Excess
Lead," Reuters, May 20, 2015, https://www.reuters.com/article/

business/healthcare-pharmaceuticals/indian-inspectors-order-recall-of
-maggi-noodles-say-found-excess-lead-idUSKBN0O51NV/.

10. Ali Tabrizi, dir., *Seaspiracy*, Netflix, 2021.

11. Kweilin Ellingrud, Saurabh Sanghvi, Gurneet Singh Dandona, et al.,
    "Generative AI and the Future of Work in America," McKinsey Global
    Institute, July 26, 2023, https://www.mckinsey.com/mgi/our-research/
    generative-ai-and-the-future-of-work-in-america.

12. United States Environmental Protection Agency, "Electric Power
    Sector Basics," https://www.epa.gov/power-sector/electric-power
    -sector-basics#:~:text=In%202021%2C%20fossil%20fuels%20
    remained,for%2021.9%25%20of%20electricity%20production.

13. Isabel Hilton, "How China Became the World's Leader on Renewable
    Energy," *Yale Environment 360,* March 13, 2024, https://e360.yale
    .edu/features/china-renewable-energy.

14. World Population Review, "Gini Coefficient by Country 2025,"
    worldpopulationreview.com/country-rankings/gini-coefficient-by
    -countryhttps://worldpopulationreview.com/country-rankings/gini
    -coefficient-by-country.

15. Karl Russell and Talmon Joseph Smith, "The Greatest Wealth Transfer
    in History Is Here, with Familiar (Rich) Winners," *New York Times,*
    May 14, 2023, https://www.nytimes.com/2023/05/14/business/
    economy/wealth-generations.html.

16. Survey conducted by author with ex-colleagues.

17. Survey conducted by author with ex-colleagues.

Chapter 5

1. Lisa Eadicicco, "WayUp Is a Booming Job-Hunting Site for
   Millennials," *Time,* May 25, 2017, https://time.com/4793254/wayup
   -jobs-career/.

2. Olivia B. Waxman, "How Internships Replaced the Entry-Level Job,"
   Time, July 25, 2018, https://time.com/5342599/history-of-interns
   -internships/.

3. John M. Nunley, Adam Pugh, Nicholas Romero, et al., "College
   Major, Internship Experience, and Employment Opportunities:

Estimates from a Resume Audit," *Labour Economics* 38 (November 2015): https://doi.org/10.1016/j.labeco.2015.11.002.

4. Katherine Schaeffer, "10 Facts About Today's College Graduates," Pew Research Center, April 12, 2022, https://www.pewresearch.org/short -reads/2022/04/12/10-facts-about-todays-college-graduates/.

5. Nunley, Pugh, Romero, et al., "College Major, Internship Experience."

6. "Glatt v. Fox Searchlight Pictures, Inc.," *Harvard Law Review* 129, no. 4 (February 2016): https://harvardlawreview.org/print/vol-129/ glatt-v-fox-searchlight-pictures-inc/.

7. United States Census Bureau, "2021 SUSB Annual Data Tables by Establishment Industry," https://www.census.gov/data/tables/2021/ econ/susb/2021-susb-annual.html.

8. Ben Rand, "The Middle Manager of the Future: More Coaching, Less Commanding," *Harvard Business Review*, February 5, 2024, https:// www.library.hbs.edu/working-knowledge/the-middle-manager-of-the -future-more-coaching-less-commanding.

9. Hugh Langley, "Google Cut Manager and VP Roles by 10% in Its Efficiency Push, CEO Sundar Pichai Said in an Internal Meeting," *Business Insider*, December 19, 2024, https://www.businessinsider .com/google-ceo-company-cut-manager-vp-roles-2024-12.

10. David Niu, "Why Middle Managers Are Secretly the Superheroes of the Workplace," *Entrepreneur*, August 23, 2016, https://www .entrepreneur.com/leadership/why-middle-managers-are-secretly-the -superheroes-of-the/280573.

11. Will Daniel, "Middle Managers Are So Burnt Out that Nearly Half Want to Quit in the Next Year," *Fortune*, February 8, 2023, https:// fortune.com/2023/02/08/work-burnout-middle-managers-nearly-half -want-to-quit-within-year/.

12. Dawn Klinghoffer and Katie Kirkpatrick-Husk, "More Than 50% of Managers Feel Burned Out," *Harvard Business Review*, May 18, 2023, https://hbr.org/2023/05/more-than-50-of-managers-feel -burned-out.

13. John Rampton, "The 6 Causes of Professional Burnout and How to Avoid Them," *Forbes*, May 13, 2015, https://www.forbes.com/sites/ johnrampton/2015/05/13/the-6-causes-of-professional-burnout-and -how-to-avoid-them; Michael Leiter and Christina Maslach, "Six

areas of worklife: A model of the organizational context of burnout," *Journal of Health and Human Services Administration*, no. 21 (Feb 1999): 472-89, https://www.researchgate.net/publication/12693291_Six_areas_of_worklife_A_model_of_the_organizational_context_of_burnout.

14. Menaka Hampole, Francesca Truffa, and Ashley Wong, "Breaking the Glass Ceiling: How MBA Programs Can Make a Big Difference," Stanford Institute for Economic Policy Research, June 2023, https://siepr.stanford.edu/publications/policy-brief/breaking-glass-ceiling-how-mba-programs-can-make-big-difference#:~:text=Figure%201%20shows%20that%20although,for%20at%20least%2015%20years.

15. "Why External Hires Get Paid More, and Perform Worse, Than Internal Staff," *Knowledge at Wharton*, March 28, 2012, https://knowledge.wharton.upenn.edu/article/why-external-hires-get-paid-more-and-perform-worse-than-internal-staff/.

16. United States Security and Exchange Commission, *Annual Report Pursuant to Section 13 or 15(D) of the Securities Exchange Act of 1934 for the Fiscal Year Ended December 31, 2024: Alphabet Inc.* (United States Security and Exchange Commission), p. 10, https://abc.xyz/assets/77/51/9841ad5c4fbe85b4440c47a4df8d/goog-10-k-2024.pdf; Ciara O'Brien, "Google in Ireland: From Small Beginnings to One of State's Biggest Private Employers," *Irish Times,* January 20, 2023, https://www.irishtimes.com/technology/2023/01/20/google-in-ireland-from-small-beginnings-to-one-of-the-countrys-biggest-private-employers/#:~:text=Tech%20giant&text=Today%2C%20Google%20employs%20more%20than,contractors%20are%20taken%20into%20account.

17. Sean Downey, "Welcome to St. John's Terminal, Our New Home in New York City," *The Keyword* (blog), February 21, 2024, https://blog.google/inside-google/life-at-google/google-nyc-st-johns-terminal-office/.

18. Charmaine Jacob, "India Stares at High Youth Unemployment as Hiring in Its Behemoth IT Sector Slows," CNBC, April 4, 2024, https://www.cnbc.com/2024/04/04/india-stares-at-high-youth-unemployment-as-hiring-in-its-it-sector-slows.html.

19. Agam Bansal, Chandan Garg, Abhijith Pakhare, et al., "Selfies: A Boon or Bane?" *Journal of Family Medicine and Primary Care* 7, no. 4 (July–August 2018): 828–31, doi: 10.4103/jfmpc.jfmpc_109_18.

20. World Economic Forum, *Future of Jobs Report 2025* (World Economic Forum, January 2025), https://reports.weforum.org/docs/ WEF_Future_of_Jobs_Report_2025.pdf.

21. James Manyika, Susan Lund, Michael Chui, et al., "Jobs Lost, Jobs Gained: What the Future of Work Will Mean for Jobs, Skills, and Wages," McKinsey Global Institute, July 16, 2024, https://www .mckinsey.com/featured-insights/future-of-work/jobs-lost-jobs-gained -what-the-future-of-work-will-mean-for-jobs-skills-and-wages.

Chapter 6

1. Sleep Junkie, "The Cities with the Highest Burnout," https://www .sleepjunkie.com/cities-with-highest-burnout/.

2. International Labor Organization, "Labor Force Survey 2023," https:// www.ilo.org/shinyapps/bulkexplorer25/?lang=en&id=EMP_TEMP_ SEX_HOW_NB_A (accessed early 2025).

3. Kathleen Wong, "Americans Are the Worst (Globally) at Taking Vacation Time: Here's How Many Days We Take," *USA Today,* June 20, 2024, https://www.usatoday.com/story/travel/2024/06/20/ americans-vacation-study-expedia-2024/74144817007/.

4. Eurydice, "Sweden: Funding in Education: Higher Education Funding," https://eurydice.eacea.ec.europa.eu/eurypedia/sweden/ higher-education-funding.

5. John F. Helliwell, Richard Layard, Jeffrey D. Sachs, et al. (eds.), *World Happiness Report, 2023* (Sustainable Development Solutions Network, 2023), https://worldhappiness.report/ed/2023/.

6. "World's Billionaires List: The Richest in 2024," *Forbes,* https://www .forbes.com/billionaires/ (accessed early 2025).

7. Cristina Enache, "Top Personal Income Tax Rates in Europe, 2023," Tax Foundation Europe, February 28, 2023, https://taxfoundation.org/ data/all/eu/top-personal-income-tax-rates-europe-2023/.

8. Enache, "Top Personal Income Tax Rates."

9. CEIC Data, "India Gross Savings Rate," https://www.ceicdata.com/en/ indicator/india/gross-savings-rate; CEIC Data, "India Posts Another Record High Trade Deficit in June," July 5, 2022, https://www .ceicdata.com/en/blog/india-posts-another-record-high-trade-deficit-june.

10. CEIC Data, "India Gross Savings Rate."

11. CEIC Data, "India Posts Another Record High Trade Deficit."

12. "Indian Household Savings Hit Half-a-Century Low as Debt Rises," *Economic Times,* September 25, 2023, https://bfsi.economictimes. indiatimes.com/news/industry/indian-household-savings-hit-half-a -century-low-as-debt-rises/103925645#:~:text=In%20terms%20 of%20actual%20numbers,13.76%20lakh%20crore%20in%202023.

13. "Indian Household Savings."

Chapter 7

1. Avshalom Caspi, "Three-Year-Old's Traits Predict Personality at Age 26," *Journal of Personality* 71, no. 4 (2003): 496–513, https:// education-consumers.org/childrens-behavioral-styles/.

2. Hailey Mensik, "A Third of Managers Harbor Unconscious Fear, Leading to $36 Billion Productivity Loss," WorkLife, November 6, 2023, https://www.worklife.news/leadership/fear-based-leadership/.

3. Mensik, "A Third of Managers."

4. Mensik, "A Third of Managers."

5. Catherine Clifford, "Google CEO: A.I. Is More Important Than Fire or Electricity," CNBC, February 1, 2018, https://www.cnbc .com/2018/02/01/google-ceo-sundar-pichai-ai-is-more-important-than -fire-electricity.html.

Chapter 8

1. Byung-Chul Han, *The Burnout Society* (Stanford University Press, 2015).

2. *State of Mobile 2025* (Sensor Tower, 2025), https://sensortower.com/ state-of-mobile-2025.

3. Alphabet Investor Relations, "Earnings," https://abc.xyz/investor/.

4. Jeff Orlowski-Yang, dir., *The Social Dilemma,* Netflix, 2020.

5. André Dua, Kweilin Ellingrud, Michael Lazar, et al., "How Does Gen Z See Its Place in the Working World? With Trepidation," McKinsey

& Company, October 19, 2022, https://www.mckinsey.com/featured
-insights/sustainable-inclusive-growth/future-of-america/how-does-gen
-z-see-its-place-in-the-working-world-with-trepidation.

6. Juliana Menasce Horowitz and Kim Parker, "How Americans View
Their Jobs," Pew Research Center, March 30, 2023, https://www
.pewresearch.org/social-trends/2023/03/30/how-americans-view-their
-jobs/.

7. "What Gen Z Graduates Want from Their Employers,"
The Economist, July 21, 2022, https://www.economist.com/
business/2022/07/21/what-gen-z-graduates-want-from-their-employers.

8. Amelia Dunlop and Michael Pankowski, "Hey Bosses: Here's What
Gen Z Actually Wants at Work," Deloitte Digital, March 26, 2023,
https://www.deloittedigital.com/us/en/insights/perspective/gen-z
-research-report.html.

9. Jack Kelly, "Gen-Z Is Labeled as 'Difficult' in the Workplace, but
There's More to the Story," *Forbes,* July 31, 2023, https://www.forbes
.com/sites/jackkelly/2023/07/31/gen-z-is-labeled-as-difficult-in-the
-workplace-but-theres-more-to-the-story/.

10. Richard Fry, "For Today's Young Workers in the U.S., Job Tenure
Is Similar to That of Young Workers in the Past," Pew Research
Center, December 2, 2022, https://www.pewresearch.org/short
-reads/2022/12/02/for-todays-young-workers-in-the-u-s-job-tenure-is
-similar-to-that-of-young-workers-in-the-past/.

11. Matt Plummer, "How to Spend Way Less Time on Email Every Day,"
Harvard Business Review, January 22, 2019, https://hbr.org/2019/01/
how-to-spend-way-less-time-on-email-every-day.

12. Cal Newport, "Email Is Making Us Miserable," *New Yorker,* February
26, 2021, https://www.newyorker.com/tech/annals-of-technology/
e-mail-is-making-us-miserable.

13. Johann Hari, *Stolen Focus: Why You Can't Pay Attention—and How
to Think Deeply Again* (Crown, 2022).

Chapter 9

1. Daniel A. Cox, "American Men Suffer a Friendship Recession,"
Survey Center on American Life, July 6, 2021, https://www

.americansurveycenter.org/commentary/american-men-suffer-a
-friendship-recession/.

2. Cox, "American Men Suffer a Friendship Recession."

3. Saloni Dattani, Lucas Rodés-Guirao, and Max Roser, "Fertility Rate," Our World in Data, 2025, https://ourworldindata.org/fertility-rate.

Rest Stop: Talk to Strangers!

1. Gillian Sandstrom and Elizabeth Dunn, "Is Efficiency Overrated?" *Social Psychological and Personality Science* 5, no. 4 (May 2014): 437–42, doi: 10.1177/1948550613502990; Joe Keohane, "Why Talking to Strangers Can Make Us Smarter," BBC, October 27, 2022, https://www.bbc.com/future/article/20221026-why-talking -to-strangers-can-make-us-happier.

2. Keohane, "Why Talking to Strangers."

3. Michael Rosenfeld, Reuben Thomas, and Sonia Hausen, "Disintermediating Your Friends: How Online Dating in the United States Displaces Other Ways of Meeting," *Proceedings of the National Academy of Sciences of the United States of America* 116, no. 36 (August 20, 2019): 17753–58, https://www.pnas.org/doi/full/10.1073/ pnas.1908630116.

Rest Stop: Build a Conscious Relationship with Technology

1. João da Silva, "Australians Get 'Right to Disconnect' After Hours," BBC, August 25, 2024, https://www.bbc.com/news/articles/ c5y32g7203vo.

Rest Stop: Embrace the Power of Incrementality and Care

1. "What Does It Mean to Be Human?" Smithsonian National Museum of Natural History, https://humanorigins.si.edu/evidence/human -fossils/species/homo-erectus; Wikipedia, s.v. "Human Evolution,"

last modified July 23, 2025, https://en.wikipedia.org/wiki/Human_
evolution.

2. Eran Galperin, "101 Gym Membership Statistics to Know," Gymdesk,
   March 2, 2025, https://gymdesk.com/blog/gym-membership-statistics/.

3. Galperin, "101 Gym Membership Statistics."

4. Galperin, "101 Gym Membership Statistics."

5. Galperin, "101 Gym Membership Statistics."

6. Galperin, "101 Gym Membership Statistics."

Rest Stop: Be Curious, Not Judgmental about Yourself

1. Emily C. Willroth, Gerald Young, Maya Tamir, et al., "Judging
   Emotions as Good or Bad: Individual Differences and Associations
   with Psychological Health," *Emotion* 23, no. 7 (October 2023):
   1876–90, doi: 10.1037/emo0001220.

2. Melinda Wenner Moyer, "Lean into Negative Emotions. It's the
   Healthy Thing to Do," *New York Times,* April 21, 2023, https://www
   .nytimes.com/2023/04/21/well/mind/negative-emotions-mental-health;
   Willroth, Young, Tamir, et al., "Judging Emotions as Good or Bad."

3. Effects of suppression, acceptance and spontaneous coping of pain
   tolerance, pain intensity and distress, *Behaviour Research and
   Therapy* vol. 45.2 (2007): 199–209. https://pubmed.ncbi.nlm.nih
   .gov/16569396/.

4. Willroth, Young, Tamir, et al., "Judging Emotions as Good or Bad."

Conclusion

1. "College Degrees Losing Edge as Graduates Find Splintered, Weaker
   US Job Market," S&P Global, November 25, 2024, https://www
   .spglobal.com/market-intelligence/en/news-insights/articles/2024/12/
   college-degrees-losing-edge-as-graduates-find-splintered-weaker-us
   -job-market-86507076#:~:text=The%20unemployment%20rate%20
   for%20US,analysis%20of%20government%20labor%20data.

ABOUT THE AUTHOR

Born and raised in Northeast India, Anmol left home at sixteen to study Economics in Mumbai. His career with Google as a behavioral researcher then took him from India to Ireland to Singapore to the United States. Throughout his corporate journey and travels around the world, he observed workplaces and societies showing similar patterns of emotional unsustainability. Along the way, he built deep connections and cultivated learning through a global network of professionals in 30+ countries across 20+ industries.

Today, Anmol channels that global experience and research into his current work: helping individuals build emotionally sustainable careers through social and personal insights. Through his coaching and consulting practice, *Wide World View,* he partners with professionals navigating burnout, career transitions, and questions of purpose.

What sets Anmol apart is his compassionate approach. He believes that while the modern workplace often demands resilience and grit, what people need just as much, if not more is an awareness of their anchors, along with vulnerability and kindness.

Whether he's working one-on-one with individuals, advising leaders, or helping shape organizational cultures, Anmol leads with a values first mindset. He meets people where they are and helps them make sense of what they truly want from work and life, by bringing a rare blend of analysis, empathy, and personal curiosity to everyone's unique life path.

With *Burnout Highway,* Anmol opens the door to a different kind of conversation about success, ambition and what it means to thrive at work. This book is just the beginning. You can learn more about his work at wideworldview.com.